Contents

About this book and the Foundation Diploma

Congratulations on your decision to take Edexcel's Foundation Diploma in Principal Learning in Creative and Media! This book will help you in all six units of your course, providing opportunities to develop functional skills, Personal, Learning and Thinking Skills, and to learn about the world of work.

There is a chapter devoted to every unit, and each chapter opens with the following:

» Overview – a description of what is covered in the unit

» Skills list – a checklist of the skills covered in the unit

» Job watch – a list of relevant careers.

This book contains many features that will help you relate your learning to the workplace and assist you in making links to other parts of the Diploma.

» Margin notes provide interesting facts and get you thinking about the industry.

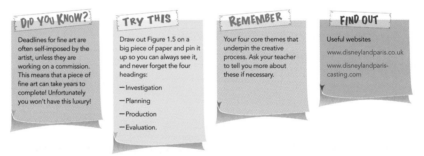

DID YOU KNOW?
Deadlines for fine art are often self-imposed by the artist, unless they are working on a commission. This means that a piece of fine art can take years to complete! Unfortunately you won't have this luxury!

TRY THIS
Draw out Figure 1.5 on a big piece of paper and pin it up so you can always see it, and never forget the four headings:
– Investigation
– Planning
– Production
– Evaluation.

REMEMBER
Your four core themes that underpin the creative process. Ask your teacher to tell you more about these if necessary.

FIND OUT
Useful websites
www.disneylandparis.co.uk
www.disneylandparis-casting.com

» Journal Tips to help you to keep a Journal of your progress.

JOURNAL TIPS
You may find that the audiences for some visual arts products have changed over the years. This is all great information to go into your Journal and Process Portfolio.

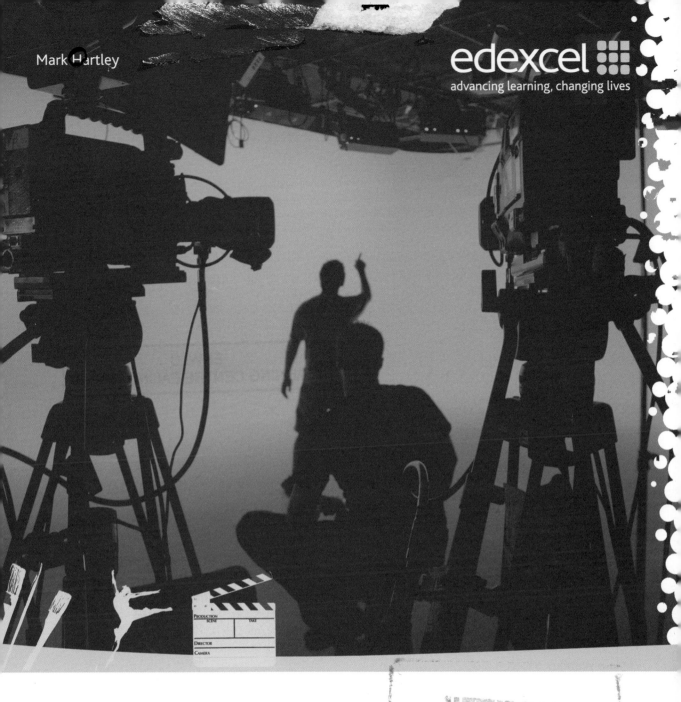

Mark Hartley

edexcel
advancing learning, changing lives

Edexcel Diploma

Creative and Media

Level 1 Foundation Diploma

Published by
Pearson Education
Edinburgh Gate
Harlow
Essex
CM20 2JE

ISBN: 978-0-435500-45-0

Picture research by Thelma Gilbert
Index by Richard Howard
Designed and typeset by Steve Moulds, DSM Partnership
Printed and bound in Great Britain at Scotprint, Haddington

Acknowledgements
The publisher would like to thank the following for their kind permission to reproduce their photographs

(key: b-bottom; c-centre; l-left; r-right; t-top)

Alamy Images: Peter Alvery 52; Avatra Images 24; Jeff Morgan 135; Picture Partners 12; **Fox FM**: 127; **Getty Images**: 123; Mark Hartley: 37, 54, 173, 175; **John Walmsley Educational**: 89; **Jupiter Unlimited**: Brand X Pictures 4 (clapboard); **Jupiterimages**: Fancy 4 (dancer); **Kobal Collection Ltd**: 10–11, 158–159, 160; **Lebrecht Music and Arts Photo Library**: 102–103; **Ben Northover**: 153; **PA Photos**: 171; **PunchStock**: Stockbyte 4 (paintbrushes); **Reuters**: 165; **Rex Features**: 38, 42–43, 47, 49, 70–71, 73, 75, 92, 132–133, 146; **Roger Scruton**: 29, 113; **Vikki Sparkes**: 97; **The Advertising Archives**: 106, 149; **William Watling**: 51, 65

Cover images: *Front*: iStockphoto: Michael Kurtz

All other images © Pearson Education

Every effort has been made to trace the copyright holders and we apologise in advance for any unintentional omissions. We would be pleased to insert the appropriate acknowledgement in any subsequent edition of this publication.

The author would like to thank the following for assistance in the writing of this book:
Adam Ball, Disneyland Paris, Carrie Grant, Henry Gray, Judy Gray, Guildford House Gallery, Gwen Hartley, Hodder & Stoughton, Leigh Hodgkinson, Kirsten Hutton (Watford Palace Theatre), Vanessa Meyer, Fiona Morey, Syd Nadim (Clock), Jo Noel-Hartley, Vikki Sparkes, Venture, Michelle Watling, Jayne Watson.

» Activities link directly to Personal, Learning and Thinking Skills and functional skills – all important parts of passing your course and vital for your future career.

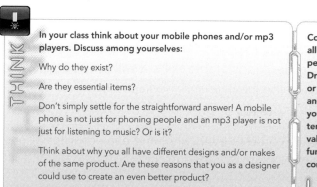

THINK

In your class think about your mobile phones and/or mp3 players. Discuss among yourselves:

Why do they exist?

Are they essential items?

Don't simply settle for the straightforward answer! A mobile phone is not just for phoning people and an mp3 player is not just for listening to music? Or is it?

Think about why you all have different designs and/or makes of the same product. Are these reasons that you as a designer could use to create an even better product?

Compare the features of all the phones owned by people in your group. Draw up a table in Word or Excel for the phones and their features. See if you can rank them in terms of things such as value for money, functionality, fashion, compactness, etc.

LINKS

» @work activities help you to think about how your learning could be applied during your work placement.

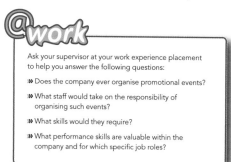

@work

Ask your supervisor at your work experience placement to help you answer the following questions:

» Does the company ever organise promotional events?

» What staff would take on the responsibility of organising such events?

» What skills would they require?

» What performance skills are valuable within the company and for which specific job roles?

» Case Study features provide a snapshot of real issues in the workplace.

Case Study

» 'I want to be…' lets you hear from real people what it is like to work in the creative and media industry.

I want to be...

Each chapter ends with Assessment Tips and an opportunity for you to check your skills and summarise what you've learned. You can also find help with technical terms in the glossary on p. 178.

Glossary terms appear in the text in **bold**.

So you want to be creative?

The Edexcel Principal Learning in Creative and Media Foundation Diploma aims to develop your creativity and confidence and your ability to think, question, explore, create and communicate, with an emphasis on gaining transferable skills. It will provide you with a basic introduction to the creative and media industry and its wide variety of job roles and skills.

For the purposes of the Foundation Diploma the creative and media industries have been divided into three groups; Art and Design, Performing Arts and Media. Each of these areas has different disciplines that you may study during your course.

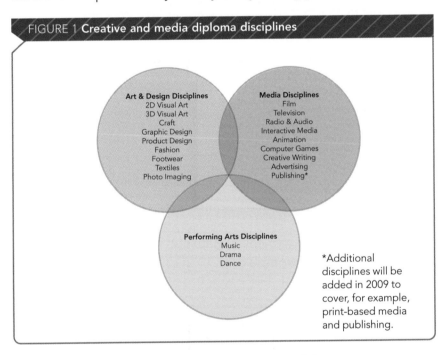

FIGURE 1 **Creative and media diploma disciplines**

Art & Design Disciplines
2D Visual Art
3D Visual Art
Craft
Graphic Design
Product Design
Fashion
Footwear
Textiles
Photo Imaging

Media Disciplines
Film
Television
Radio & Audio
Interactive Media
Animation
Computer Games
Creative Writing
Advertising
Publishing*

Performing Arts Disciplines
Music
Drama
Dance

*Additional disciplines will be added in 2009 to cover, for example, print-based media and publishing.

Which disciplines you study will be a matter of discussion between you and your teachers, but you will have to study the minimum of six disciplines over the whole course from the minimum of two areas.

However, for the Edexcel Foundation Diploma you have the chance within Unit 1 to experience all areas of the creative and media industry – Art and Design, Performing Arts and Media. This will give you an excellent opportunity to be introduced to all areas of the industry, which will help you to decide which two to concentrate on for this diploma and will also benefit your later understanding of more specific disciplines.

Qualification structure

Figure 2 shows the units you will cover during your course. After Unit 1, you will choose whether to study two or three of the following three units. Your teachers at your **centre** will help you to decide.

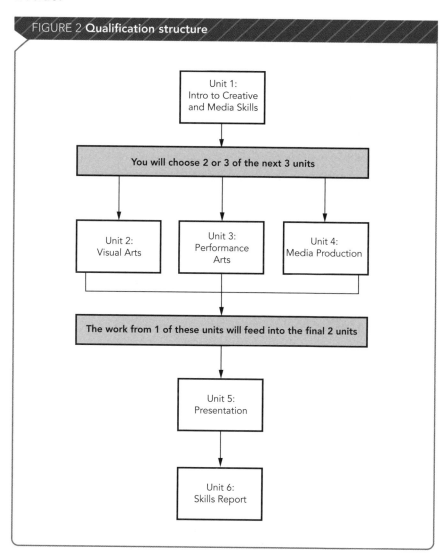

FIGURE 2 **Qualification structure**

Unit 1:
Intro to Creative
and Media Skills

You will choose 2 or 3 of the next 3 units

Unit 2:
Visual Arts

Unit 3:
Performance
Arts

Unit 4:
Media Production

The work from 1 of these units will feed into the final 2 units

Unit 5:
Presentation

Unit 6:
Skills Report

Diploma themes

Common to all the clusters, disciplines and units is the *creative process*, which we will look at in more detail during Unit 1. However the creative process is underpinned by four themes outlined over the page.

TRY THIS

Is your work is good enough? You must learn to be objective. Think about all the people auditioning for *X-Factor* or *Britain's Got Talent*. Are they good at being objective about their own skills and abilities?

DID YOU KNOW?

These generic skills are regarded as transferable skills because you use them in all different walks of life. If you moved out of creative and media completely, these are the sorts of skills that you would still need in your new career.

» **Creativity in context** – about knowing how your surroundings in everyday life can change or be changed by the creative and media industries.

» **Thinking and working creatively** – about developing an environment in which to be creative, so you can think and work effectively.

» **Principles, processes and practice** – about developing the practical skills and techniques that are at the heart of the creative process, including theoretical knowledge important to all disciplines and an awareness of health and safety.

» **Creative business and enterprise** – about being business and market aware. Even if you work for yourself you are still running your own business. Being creative will mean nothing if you can't be heard, seen or pay your bills.

Every unit you will study will cover these core themes although the emphasis may change from unit to unit.

Skills for life

This qualification is future proof! Its emphasis is on the fundamental skills of understanding the industry and being creative. It will show you how to continue to develop and learn new skills and techniques well after you have left education and moved into work. You should never stop learning!

Technology in the creative and media industry advances very fast, so you need to know how to keep up – be passionate and ready for anything. Employment is changing, too. People are not staying in the same job with the same company for very long. A few generations ago people would typically be with the same company for decades, with some progression within the company. Now people commonly jump from one company to other or switch between departments to improve their career with much more rapid changes in job role. As your career progresses you may find you have a portfolio of jobs. If you are freelance you will continually have to create the next job by chasing leads and networking.

So you can see that the industry requires its workforce to be flexible and adaptable, and prepared to transfer its creative skills into any job role. You will experience this within the Foundation Diploma when you start working on a project and find that many disciplines overlap. You need to be open-minded and happy to give anything a go to be successful on this course.

You will also find that this course gives you opportunities to acquire and develop generic skills. These are functional skills in English, ICT and mathematics and personal, learning and thinking skills (PLTS).

Process Portfolio and Journal

For each of the first four units you will be asked to compile a Process Portfolio. Your teachers will give you guidance on what to include depending on the assignment you are working on. We will talk more about this in Unit 1, but typically, a Process Portfolio will include your notes on: research, generation and development of creative ideas, decision making, planning and evaluation.

You will also be asked to record the creative process within a journal or logbook (for the rest of the book we will simply refer to it as your Journal, or in Unit 2, your sketchbook) that will become part of your Process Portfolio. Within the units we will give you ideas on how to record the creative and production processes and what to include. Your Journal and other parts of your Process Portfolio can be presented in many different forms, from traditional notebooks to videos and online blogs.

Your Process Portfolio is vital to your receiving the grades you deserve! Without a detailed and thoughtful portfolio supporting your final piece of work the examiners will simply not be able to properly judge your abilities. You will also need a detailed Process Portfolio to complete Unit 6: Skills Report.

And finally...

Being creative is relatively easy, creativity is part of being human: being creative in the commercial world is difficult. This is where this course can help. It will give you the tools you need to start on the road to a successful creative and media career.

We hope you enjoy using this book, and we wish you the very best for your Diploma course and your future in the creative and media industry.

> **REMEMBER**
>
> Be thorough and disciplined and ensure you keep detailed notes of the processes you go through to create your creative and media products.

> **REMEMBER**
>
> Trust within the group studying on this qualification is really important. Help create a supportive environment where everyone is allowed to make mistakes, but learn from them!

OVERVIEW

This unit is designed to introduce you to the three main areas of the creative and media industries, so that you can understand how they all relate and link with each other. It also helps you to assess your skills and weaknesses and offers advice on how to improve your learning techniques, both at school or college and in your future career.

As you work through this unit you will carry out three modules, one for each of the following three areas of the industry:

» visual arts

» performance arts

» media production.

These will give you a practical taste of the kinds of work you might be doing for the rest of the course. This experience of the three areas will include looking at job opportunities and pathways within the industry.

The unit will concentrate first on helping improve the way you learn, which will not only help you to achieve this unit, but also ensure you are skilled and prepared for the rest of the course.

We have made this guidance as industry-based and relevant to the real world as possible. Skills you will learn and improve upon include report writing and the preparation and giving of presentations. Competence in these areas is vital in the creative and media sectors, and can often make the difference between securing work from a client or not.

Common to all sectors, disciplines and units is something called the creative process which is underpinned by four core themes: creativity in context; thinking and working creatively; principles, processes and practice; and creative business and enterprise.

01

Introduction to Creative and Media Skills

Skills list

At the end of this unit you should:

» be able to apply skills required to enable effective learning and thinking

» know how to carry out basic research in the creative and media sector

» be able to apply skills needed by those working in the creative and media sector

» know some job roles and career paths in the creative and media sector.

Job watch

Job roles in the creative and media industry include:

» visual arts – painter, sculptor, textiles artist, graphic designer, product designer, fashion designer, photographer

» performance arts – actor, singer, dancer, musician, composer, director, choreographer

» media production – film and television producer, radio producer, web designer, animator, computer games designer, advertising/marketing manager, writer.

Applying skills to effective learning and thinking

Before we start looking at the skills you will need for a career in creative and media, let's check out some more basic skills – ones you probably never even think about – those of **learning** and how to become your own best teacher.

From the minute we are born to the day we die, we are naturally learning. Unfortunately some people have negative learning experiences during their lives and can lose the passion to learn and acquire new skills. The secret is to understand how we each learn, and give ourselves every opportunity to learn effectively.

When we are babies and small children we learn by watching, copying and doing. When we get to school, however, the way we learn changes, moving gradually from play and experience to being actively taught by teachers and finally to simply receiving information – for instance in lectures.

FIGURE 1.1 **As babies we learn by experience**

As we get used to being told what to do and what to learn by our teachers it can be easy to lose the most important skill of all, the ability to study what is going on around us and learn for ourselves, without someone else telling or teaching us. To be successful in this diploma, or in other higher qualifications, and in the world of work, you need to become confident, skilled and *independent* learners. That means you learn how to learn on your own. If you want a successful and long-lasting career you must be happy with change and the challenges you face, and be able to continually learn new skills and develop old ones.

REFLECT

Imagine you have completed your creative and media course where you learnt to use the latest media equipment and software. You get a job in the industry, but the technology you use changes quickly. What are you going to do? If you don't have the ability to self-teach you could easily find yourself getting left behind as equipment becomes outdated and replaced by new technologies.

Try out a new piece of computer software or try and find some new functions in a program you alredy use.

LINKS

Attitudes to learning

We want you to have the skills to successfully complete this and the other units, and develop skills that you can use for the rest of your life. In order for this to happen, you need to develop the right attitudes to learning. Approach things **rationally** and **objectively** and always be prepared to question your judgement. Be open to new ideas and be willing to learn from others.

Studying does not only mean reading books! Many professionals will tell you that they learned most about creativity and techniques by watching and 'studying' others. Working alongside an 'old pro' (professional) on stage or in a media or art studio, for example, will be invaluable to you. Watch and learn and work out what it is that makes them good.

It is good to be confident in your work and abilities, but it is equally important to remember that you will never know everything, however successful you become. You should always remain open to learning. Peter Jones, the multi-millionaire businessman who featured on TV's *Dragons' Den*, talks about the importance of this for potential tycoons:

> 'It is crucial not to become overconfident, as this can lead to complacency and arrogance. Contrary to popular belief, the Tycoon is not an arrogant specimen. Quite the opposite. Confident, yes, but all Tycoons feel they are still learning. Arrogance means you think you know it all and act accordingly. The Tycoon is hungry to learn, always.'

Peter Jones
Tycoon (2007),
Hodder & Stoughton

In summary, to be your own best teacher you need to remember to:

» learn from studying others

» approach learning in a rational and objective way

» always ask yourself why

» be confident, but not arrogant, and remain ready to learn!

What type of learner are you?

Thankfully we are not all the same! If we were then the world would be very dull indeed, especially within the creative and media industry. Imagine if all TV companies broadcast the same programmes, with the same format and content, or if all bands produced the same style of music and all art galleries were filled with the same kinds of painting!

We are not all the same in the way we learn, either, and one of the first things for you to do is to work out what kind of learner you are. You will know from your experience at school that kids fall into different categories: there are sporty kids, book worms, arty kids and some kids that can't seem to stop singing or dancing! These sorts of preferences also reflect what kind of learner you are.

If you struggle with learning something, it's easy to write it off as being something that doesn't interest you. However, it could be that the way you are trying to learn it doesn't match your individual style, and this is what makes it so hard. Let's start by finding out what kind of learner you are.

Learner-type assessment
The table to the right has four groups of activities or items. Look down the lists and tick which of them you like or agree with. Tick as many as you want from any of the groups. There are no right or wrong answers.

TABLE 1.1 Learning types

Group 1	Group 2
Do you like:	Do you like:
☐ charts	☐ phoning people
☐ maps	☐ discussions
☐ graphs	☐ arguments/debates
☐ pictures	☐ story tellers
☐ diagrams	☐ meetings
☐ drawing	☐ talking
☐ looking at art	☐ poetry read aloud
☐ field trips?	☐ discussion groups?
☐ Is the look of an object, such as a magazine or album cover, important or interesting to you?	☐ Do you believe what others say? ☐ Are you impressed by people who speak well in public?

Group 3	Group 4
Do you like:	Do you like:
☐ lists	☐ to use all your senses
☐ dictionaries	☐ examples
☐ definitions	☐ tours/trips
☐ minutes of meetings	☐ 'getting your hands dirty'
☐ handouts	☐ trial and error
☐ print resources, for example newspapers, books, magazines, websites	☐ field trips
☐ quotations	☐ practical exercises
☐ reading poetry	☐ using social networking sites or interactive media?
☐ contracts	
☐ reports	☐ Do you prefer to make a decision to buy something only after using it and trying it out?
☐ taking notes?	
☐ Do you agree that if it's not in print then it can't be believed?	

So what kind of learner are you? (See table to left.) If you have got ticks in every group then you learn using all the senses, although you might lean more towards one or another. Most learners have a preference for two areas, for example Visual and Do. Some learners have a firm preference for just one area.

The most important thing about doing this exercise is not the number of ticks, but getting you to think about how you prefer to learn. What we need to do is make sure that your preferred learning style doesn't prevent you from learning the skills you need for your career.

Suppose you are a Visual and Do learner, for instance, listening to a teacher in class and making notes could be hard for you. So what can you do to compensate or improve your skills to listen and write? You might consider making **concept maps** instead of taking verbal notes in lessons. Or you could follow up lessons with some practical exercises to practise the theory covered by the teacher. If you are an Aural learner, why not use a Dictaphone or voice recorder to make notes. Try to discuss lessons after the class with other learners to help you remember what was said.

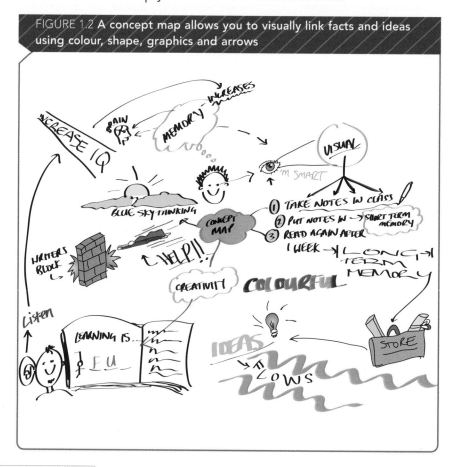

FIGURE 1.2 **A concept map allows you to visually link facts and ideas using colour, shape, graphics and arrows**

MANAGE

Look at your learning strengths and draw up a list of activities or resources that you should use every day to help your learning. Try to expand the list by considering other things that could help. For example if you are a Visual learner, the use of visual cues, such as Post-it notes, highlighter pens and wall charts, will improve you learning.

Consider your weaker areas. What can you do to improve them? Luckily for you the disciplines you might study on this course could be of great help – for example, music and singing should improve your aural skills.

LINKS

Create a table displaying your learning strengths and the activities or resources, using headings for the columns and rows.

Skills audit

How do you know what you need to learn? Well, sometimes this is obvious, for instance if you have to learn how to use a new piece of equipment or software for your job. If you work in a large company then you may be trained in the new skills required. However, we don't always know what our needs are. So how do you assess your skill needs?

Professional companies within any industry will carry out **skills audits**. These allow them to see what skills their employees have and what skills they need to develop to ensure the company remains competitive in the future. If you work for yourself, then the ability to do your own skills audits to evaluate your strengths and weaknesses is crucial to survive in the competitive world of work.

JOIN IN

Many actors list additional skills and interests on their CV. This list is important to casting directors. For example if an actor needs to be able to ride a horse or play golf for a scene in a film, production schedules are often too tight for the actor to learn these skills, so only actors who have stated that they can ride a horse or play golf on their CV will make it through to audition. Be careful not to exaggerate you talents though – many actors have been caught out and had to do a crash course in something like horse riding!

If you are a budding actor, it would be sensible to keep up some of the sports and extra-curricular activities and interests that so many young people give up when they get to GCSEs or A Levels. Make a list of all your past and present skills and interests. Choose one or two to keep up to scratch, or even investigate a new interest. Join a local or college club and improve your skills.

Now, you probably don't realise that you have regularly had skills audits at school or college. You might know them as tutorials or reviews with your teachers, sometimes involving your parents.

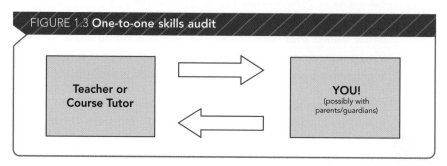

FIGURE 1.3 **One-to-one skills audit**

You could argue that the teacher doesn't know what you're really like, or that they don't know the full picture of your talents and commitment, as they can only judge you from what they see within the school environment. They might not take into account your successes in extra-curricular activities in and out of school, your part-time job, voluntary work, and so on. Well, the industry would agree with you that this kind of skills audit is limited and doesn't reflect the pressures of working in a competitive industry where so many other people will judge your ability.

To be successful you not only need to consider what your boss (or teacher) thinks of you, but the people you are working with, the people that you are working for and, most importantly, the quality of your work. In business this is called '360-degree feedback', and it is where you acquire feedback from everyone that comes into contact with you during your job. This could be your boss, your colleagues, clients, audience and customers. All these people will have an opinion on how you do your job. Whatever comments they have, whether critical, constructive or supportive, you will need to evaluate them if you are going to improve your performance. To improve, you need to look at where your skills, or lack of them, are preventing you from doing a better job.

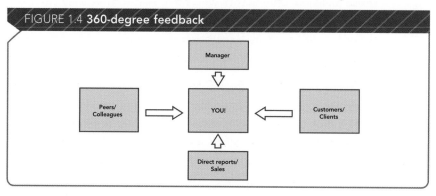

FIGURE 1.4 **360-degree feedback**

Carry out your own skills audit

Let's now look at what skills you think you have already. The skills audit suggested here is one you can repeat regularly throughout your working life, not only to make sure you are increasing your skill base, but also to see where your needs have changed.

A skills audit can be very detailed – ask you teacher to show you examples, but for now try to consider the particular skills of relevance to this qualification.

REFLECT

Copy out and complete the following table about your skills at the beginning of the course. We have given you one example for each to give you an idea (don't worry if you have very little to write at the moment).

TABLE 1.2 **Skills audit**

	Personal Evidence	Skills Gained
Art & Design	Attended extra-curricular art classes at school – made a mug out of clay	Can make something out of clay, understand the techniques involved to ensure it doesn't crack during firing
Performing Arts	Attended dance classes for two years outside school	Can tap dance to level 2
Media Production	Family bought a new Apple computer for home – edited family holiday video and made a DVD and sent the file via email to family abroad	Can use iMovie & iDVD Can save edited movies as QuickTime for sending via email

The exciting part is when you come to complete a skills audit at the end of the course – it should be very different with lots to write about!

When you apply for jobs, companies often send a Person Specification, a list of essential and desirable skills and experience required. This is a great opportunity for you to carry out a skills audit of yourself, matching you current skills and **competencies** against those of the job role. It will help you to analyse where you need to learn new skills or develop old ones, and even decide whether or not the job is one you should be applying for!

Journals and Process Portfolios

In all units you are required as part of your assessment to keep a log, or journal. This offers an account of what you have done, and also forms important evidence of your progress and understanding. We will refer to this as your Journal throughout.

Your Journal should contain information about the development of your work and ideas during the course. When it is assessed your teacher will want to see that you have been reflective and demonstrate you understand how the things you have learned have influenced your approach to your work.

Many learners starting to write their Journal simply write down what they did and when. However this is not enough. Your Journal should be **analytical** rather than descriptive, and be something you can use to reflect on and learn from. Don't waste time describing activities and lessons in detail, your teacher knows what they taught you! Just make brief notes to remind yourself of what you did. Concentrate instead on ideas, how you felt about each task, what worked and what didn't, and what your strengths and weaknesses were.

This process is called **evaluation**. If you always consider 360-degree feedback when evaluating your work (what your teacher thought, what your class or team-mates thought, and so on) then it will be much easier to think of things to talk about and gather evidence of your learning!

As you work through this book we will help you with writing an effective Journal for specialist areas of the industry. We will also look at different ways to approach your Journal to make it easier for working in different disciplines.

Process Portfolio

You will also be expected to keep a Process Portfolio of all relevant documents illustrating the creative and developmental processes you go through. Your teacher will tell you more about this.

Your Process Portfolio for this unit may include a business report and/or proposal. You must also include all the paperwork from meetings, research materials, notes – everything to back up your decision-making.

Being creative and productive

Your diploma course is designed to help you learn about the creative and media industry by doing and experiencing it rather than just reading about it. This is called **experiential learning** – or learning by experience.

When you complete a task, you should be able to review what you have done, learn from where it went well, where it didn't go well and where things could have been done differently. You should then use your knowledge and skills to plan your next attempt more successfully.

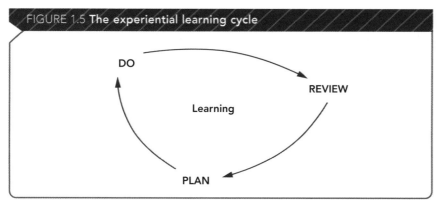

FIGURE 1.5 **The experiential learning cycle**

The creative process

The creative process, or cycle, is fundamental to everything you will ever do during this course and within the creative and media industries.

These stages are all important for any successful media production, be it a piece of art or design, some performance art, an exhibition or any other media product.

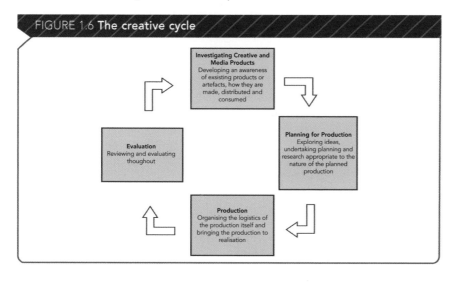

FIGURE 1.6 **The creative cycle**

TRY THIS

Draw out Figure 1.6 on a big piece of paper and pin it up so you can always see it, and never forget the four headings:

● Investigation

● Planning

● Production

● Evaluation.

Carrying out basic research in the creative and media sector

You'll see from Figure 1.6 that research is an important part of both the investigation and planning of a media production. The word 'research' might make you think of stuffy old men with small round glasses wearing tweed jackets with elbow pads and reading dusty old books in a library! But don't be fooled, research is vital for the success of your media product. It also isn't dry and dusty! Research can include anything from surfing the net to going to the cinema – think of it more as information gathering, and you get the idea. Everyone carries out research, from the artist desperate to sell a painting to the TV producer developing the next Saturday night primetime show. Both need to research the market so they know what their customers want. But research is not just about knowing your market, it can also provide the foundations of your creative ideas!

Creative thinking

Being able to think creatively is an essential skill in this industry. But we can't expect ideas to just drop into our laps – they have to come from somewhere. We are all influenced by our experiences and what goes on around us. You need to be able to harness that experience and use it to inform your ideas and creative thinking. If you know you need to come up with some ideas on a particular theme or for a particular project, it's a good idea to research some background information first. This will help you put ideas into context and will get your mind attuned to the subject you need to come up with ideas about. If you go to a meeting to discuss new ideas for a project with no research, you will be able respond with how you feel about the ideas, but not to make an informed judgement. Doing some research or investigation first gives you the information to allow you to reach reasoned conclusions and make informed decisions.

Creative thinking processes

You will hear a lot of talk in the industry about 'blue sky thinking' or thinking 'out of the box'. This is when you come up with ideas without taking into account any preconceptions or prejudices, and don't instantly dismiss any ideas.

TEAMWORK

Why not try out having a 'blue sky meeting' with your fellow learners? Choose a creative problem that needs solving, such as how the college could advertise or market the course you are on.

Be disciplined and follow these guidelines:

1. Select a room that allows everyone in the team to be seen and heard.

2. Organise a large whiteboard or flipchart to write the ideas generated from the group on.

3. Make sure whoever is writing up the ideas does not favour any particular view and allows everyone to have an equal say.

4. State the creative problem clearly, and invite ideas.

5. When someone offers an idea, wait until they have fully explained it before writing on the board so no one is distracted. Write only a short summary of the idea on the board – this could be simply one word.

6. **Do not** allow anyone to comment on any of the ideas at this stage! But if an idea is not fully understood then ask for clarification.

7. Only when all the flow of ideas stops should you then change coloured pens and go around each idea considering its strengths and weaknesses. You can jump about from one idea to another, as someone making a comment on one idea may stimulate discussion on another. Again **no** idea should be dismissed at this point.

8. Only when everyone has aired all their ideas and discussed the pros and cons fully, should you start to discuss which ideas are not practical and which are possibilities.

At the end of your meeting you may still not be able to decide on the best idea. This is where research and investigation comes in again. You need to follow up the best ideas and find out how feasible they are before making a final decision. Many companies will spend a good deal of time trying out two or three ideas before eventually deciding on one.

Think about making opportunities to allow others to speak.

Did you listen effectively? Could you summarise what people said?

LINKS

Many companies will have creative meetings where a team of people will have to '**idea storm**'– that is come up with lots of creative ideas to solve a problem or answer a question. You may have experienced 'brain storming' lessons similar to this. During these sessions it is really important to discipline yourself not to dismiss others' ideas straight away, no matter how ridiculous you might think they are at first. For truly amazing and innovative ideas to be aired, everyone in the group needs to feel comfortable about saying what they are thinking, without the worry of being laughed at. Many people laughed at James Dyson when he first suggested a vacuum cleaner without a bag, but his company is now as famous as Hoover, one of the original and best-known vacuum cleaner companies (with bags!).

Idea storming sessions are not intended to come up with the whole solution. You may have a great idea, but you don't necessarily know how to make it happen. The important thing is that sharing these ideas in a supportive environment can mean that someone else might have the solution to make your idea a reality.

FIGURE 1.7 **Creative meetings encourage the flow of ideas and blue sky thinking**

The research process

Once you have your ideas for your media product you need to be disciplined in the process of turning an idea into reality through good solid research.

Primary and secondary research

There are two types of research that you might carry out – primary and secondary. Primary research is original information gained from finding things out for yourself, secondary research is what someone else has found out.

TABLE 1.3 **Primary and secondary research**	
1. Primary	**2. Secondary**
Site visits	The Internet
Interviews	Books
Questionnaires and surveys	Newspapers, journals and magazines
Appraisal of existing creative and media products	Television and radio programmes

THINK

What factors do you think might affect the reliability of:
– primary research
– secondary research?

Find a piece of secondary research on the Internet. Create a Word file and write a short account about how you found it and how reliable you think it is.

LINKS

Primary research can take longer and you don't always have the time or the physical resources to use primary research methods all the time. Also, you may not have the expertise to attempt some types of primary research and will gain more insights if you refer to research done by people who are more expert or knowledgeable than yourself. You can still have opinions on their work and draw your own conclusions from their findings. Most professionals will use a combination of both primary and secondary research.

Research and investigation skills

Compiling a brief
Before you start researching and investigating it is a good idea to compile your own brief so you are absolutely focused on what you need to achieve. You should include:

» your **aims** and **objectives**

» available resources, both for research and production

» actions needed to meet objectives

» who is involved

» deadlines.

Identifying research tasks

Plan the research you will carry out and consider the resources available. Here are some useful guidelines:

1. Write down everything you know about the idea already.

2. Identify sources of evidence that support your views or decisions.

3. Identify the gaps in your knowledge.

4. Write down what you need to know – bullet points.

5. Identify sources for each point – where are you going to find the information?

6. Consider the available resources, books, Internet, DVDs, CDs, academic journals, magazines, TV and so on, then investigate how you will access these resources. Will your school library have all the books you need, for instance, or will you have to go to a larger or specialist library?

Recording your sources

As you start to gather information, you must note where it has come from. Keep a record of all the web pages, books and magazines you use, and make sure you link all the information you find with its source. If you photocopy some pages from a book, for instance, make sure you write the title, author and date of the book on the photocopy so that you know where the pages are from. This is for two reasons. The first is to ensure you can prove that your work is your own and that you have not **plagiarised** anything, and the second is to ensure that your decisions are properly supported and referenced.

It would be very embarrassing, for instance, for a professional to argue in an important meeting that the company should make a particular decision based on some specific figures, but when challenged couldn't say where the figures came from.

Similarly, it would be a real shame if you explained in your assessment work for this qualification all the decisions you came to and why, but there was no evidence that you had done any research. This would make it very difficult for your work to achieve the higher grades and it might also make you vulnerable to being accused of plagiarism.

What is plagiarism?

Plagiarism is a form of cheating. It is claiming someone else's work, thoughts or ideas, as your own. This can be copying something word for word from a book or website without permission and presenting it as your own work. It is still plagiarism if the person whose work you are copying gives you their permission, but you do not acknowledge it. Therefore if you copy work, in whole or part, or if you download pages from the Internet into a report and don't reference it, you are cheating. It's very easy to reference your sources. You just have to clearly state where the piece of text has come from, who wrote it and when. It is no defence to claim ignorance or say you did it by accident.

All schools and colleges will have a policy on plagiarism that will involve quite serious disciplinary action if anyone is caught. Most universities will ask you to leave, so it is sensible to get into good habits now by simply making sure that you have a list of the resources you used to research your product, and that you reference particular quotes or sections of text that you write out without changing into your own words.

There is nothing wrong with using quotes from your sources. Someone else who is a lot more experienced than you probably explains something much better in their own words than you could ever rewrite it. Just make sure you make it very clear who originally wrote or said the quote, and when and where you found it. Look back at the quote by Peter Jones on page 13. You will see that we have credited him personally and put the source of the quotation.

What is a bibliography?

A bibliography is traditionally a list of sources at the back of a book or essay showing where the research has come from. However, not all research comes from books these days. There are discographies for CDs, records and tapes, and videographies for videos and DVDs. You might find you also need to list websites, TV programmes, films, radio broadcasts and so on. If you want to reference information given to you personally, for instance from a conversation, email or letter, you can do this too. Just record the date, the name of the person and indicate it was a personal communication or 'pers. comm.'.

The usual way to display the information for a book in a bibliography is:

Author's Surname, First Name. (Year of Publication or Copyright) *Title*, Name of Publisher: Place of Publication. ISBN

e.g.
Hartley, Mark (2008) *Creative and Media Level 1 Foundation Diploma*, Pearson Education: Harlow. ISBN: 978-0-435-50045-0

You can list discographies and videographies in a similar way.

e.g.
Name of Artiste. *Name of CD or Video*. Place of Record/Production Company: Record/Production Company Name, Date of Recording.

If possible, try to list the recording date rather than the copyright dates as when a song or video was recorded is usually much more interesting for your research than when a particular CD was released or re-released.

Research sources

Once you have got your ideas and identified your tasks, you will need to start gathering information through research and investigation. So where are you going to look?

The Internet

The Internet will be one of your main sources. In the space of only fifteen or so years, the Internet has changed our world for ever, making many research tasks and investigations hugely quicker to carry out than before. No more hoofing round libraries, just enter a term in Google and the information is at your fingertips! However, you must be careful. Information in books and journals has often been checked and refereed by experts before it ever got to print. The same is not true of the Internet. Anyone can put anything up on the Internet so it cannot always be trusted to be completely accurate. It's not just self-regulated sites such as Wikipedia that are prone to vandals; many sites look as though they are an authority on a subject, but actually have few credentials to back up their claims. So be careful in quoting some websites that may just be a collection of someone's unsupported feelings on a subject – this is hardly going to give your work the credibility you need. Company websites usually produce some excellent information that would benefit you in your investigations, but often you may find it far more reliable to use the web to find a phone number for a company and phone them for information, rather than trust facts and figures from a dodgy website! It is also vitally important you do not lose the skills of verbal communication and don't rely completely on email and the Internet.

FIGURE 1.8 **You will need to refer to lots of different secondary sources in your research**

Printed sources

If you need to get historical information then it is probably better to use good old-fashioned books. Published books, magazines, journals and newspapers are rigorously monitored; if a publisher prints information that is incorrect then an expensive legal case could follow, so it's in their best interests to get things right. These publications are therefore much more dependable for your research.

Primary sources

One of the best ways to find something out is to ask someone who knows. It can be quite scary at times to interview someone, but if you are prepared with sensible questions it can be incredibly valuable.

However, for many things in the creative arts, people's opinions are **subjective** – one piece of artwork, a TV show or piece of music may be loved by some and hated by others. Therefore in the creative and media world we will often conduct questionnaires so we can ask more than one person's opinion. If when we carry out this research we also ask questions about their background, age and so on, we can also develop an understanding of our audience.

Note taking

Remember note taking is not just for the classroom. Most professionals will spend a good deal of their time noting their ideas so they don't forget them. You may want to record the content of an interview or the proceedings of a meeting, something you heard on the radio, information from a gallery or exhibition, or even an idea that came to you as you were sitting on the bus! Some creative and media professionals keep their notebooks for many years, as they constantly refer back to them.

There are two different types of note taking: linear notes and pattern notes. With linear note taking you list your notes as you make them. It helps to number them so that they are grouped together. For example, if you are note taking in a meeting you will start with 1, as a note for the main question or idea you are discussing, you would then use 1.1, 1.2, 1.3 and so on for any notes relating to this question or idea. If the meeting changes direction and you start talking about something different then you can change to 2, 2.1, 2.2, 2.3 etc.

FIGURE 1.9 **An example of linear notes**

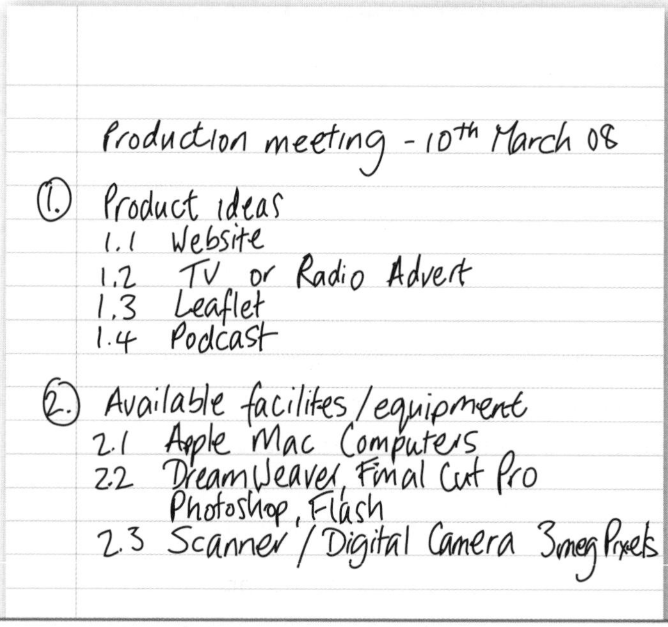

Production meeting – 10th March 08
1. Product ideas
   1.1 Website
   1.2 TV or Radio Advert
   1.3 Leaflet
   1.4 Podcast

2. Available facilites / equipment
   2.1 Apple Mac Computers
   2.2 DreamWeaver, Final Cut Pro
          Photoshop, Flash
   2.3 Scanner / Digital Camera 3meg Pixels

Pattern notes are similar to the concept maps you draw when you have idea storms. You write the idea or question you are discussing or researching in the middle of the page and then write ideas around it, sometimes using different colours, boxes, lines and arrows to link different aspects. You have to make sure you leave space around the entries so that you can fit everything in.

FIGURE 1.10 **An example of pattern notes**

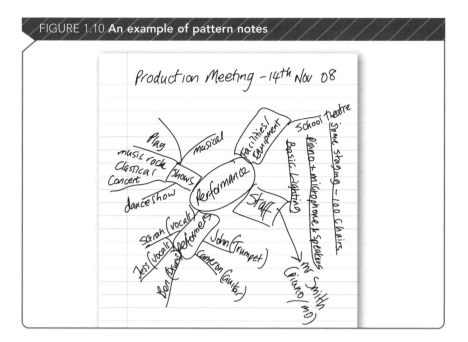

Pattern notes are a useful learning aid for people who prefer to learn visually.

Remember the following to help you be more proficient and make the most of your notes later on:

» Date the page and number subsequent pages.

» Use different coloured pens and highlighters to link related information. You remember information better in colour.

» Use abbreviations to speed up your note taking – but remember the abbreviations! Keep a list in the back of your notebook.

» Don't simply write everything down that is said in meetings and rehearsals! There will often be a lot of discussion so keep your notes succinct. Only record what is decided, bullet point ideas or even draw diagrams and/or pictures.

» Use a bound notebook rather than individual sheets, as these can easily get separated and lost. Professionals often use an A5 hard-backed notebook. This is sturdy and its size makes it easy to carry so you are more likely to always have it with you.

Presenting your research

In the real world, once you have done your research you need to present it to your boss or your client – drawing conclusions from what you have found out and making proposals as appropriate.

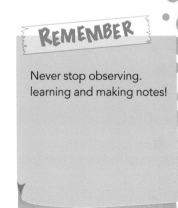

REMEMBER

Never stop observing. learning and making notes!

This may take the form of a business report or proposal or a presentation. For your diploma, you also need to present the results of your research in your Process Portfolio. Less formally, you could present your research as a **blog**.

Reports and proposals

The key difference between something you write for school and something you write for business is that your teacher has to read your essay. A busy business executive reading your report or proposal doesn't have to read it, especially if it is uninteresting and long-winded. Therefore you need to develop a writing style that is succinct, accurate, well laid-out and that clearly states any definite conclusions. To make sure your writing is effective and businesslike, follow these basic guidelines:

1. Ensure that the content is in a logical order.

2. Use headings, sub-headings and bullet points to organise the material.

3. Be succinct – don't waffle or write in long unbroken paragraphs.

4. Stick to the subject, don't go off at a tangent.

5. Don't draw conclusions without evidence.

6. Proofread your work, get someone else to check it, and then check it again!

Two types of business writing you should know about are business reports and business proposals. You also need to understand how to put together your own Process Portfolio.

Business reports

A business report tends to have a very simple, three-part structure:

» Introduction – this should grab the attention of the reader, lay out the purpose of the report and summarise the main conclusions.

» Body – this outlines your method and findings, providing the evidence to support your conclusions and recommendations.

» Conclusions and/or recommendations – this should concisely lay out the conclusions you reach, and your recommendations for action based on those conclusions.

Business proposals

A business proposal is a suggestion for a business activity, for example money-raising to fund a musical theatre show, or the designing of a new corporate identity for a company. It aims to put a sound business case, both financially and strategically, and to outline how the project will be carried out.

» Introduction – sets out the project.

» Explanation – why the project is needed and what it contributes to the company, audience, client or customer.

» Estimate of resources – financial breakdown or budget.

» Staffing – who is responsible and who will undertake the work.

» Timescale.

» Plan of action/**production schedule**.

Presentations

A presentation takes exactly the same amount of research, planning, preparation and organisation as a report. The ability to present well is crucial for many jobs within the creative and media industry, but it can be difficult at first.

Visual aids

Visual aids make the presentation more interesting and can help to explain concepts. They also help you to remember what you have got to say. Visual aids should support what you are saying, hopefully in an exciting or engaging way – pictures, diagrams and bullet points can help reinforce your message. Visuals can be as simple as a flipchart or some pictures you might hold up. Visual display software applications, such PowerPoint, can help you to present your work in a professional way and are especially good for helping you organise and structure your talk. However PowerPoint presentations can also be used very badly, even by experienced people. They should never be your written report simply divided up on slides that you read out to your audience!

Here are some do's and don'ts of making presentations and using PowerPoint to help prevent you sending your audience to sleep:

TABLE 1.4 Do's and don'ts in giving a presentation	
DO	**DON'T**
• script and rehearse – you need to know what you are saying and what's coming up next	• use too much text on slides – single words or bullets are far more effective. If your audience has too much to read they will stop listening
• use large, clear text so the audience can read it from a distance	• read every word from a script or the PowerPoint slides
• use hand gestures and be physically expressive! Your enthusiasm and passion for the subject will rub off on your audience	• use flashy animations, graphics and sound effects that might slow your presentation down. Good creative design is usually quite simple. Make your presentation clever and intelligent, not cluttered and tacky
• speak much slower and louder than you usually would talk	
• look at your audience, make eye contact	• say sorry or apologise for things, this shows you are nervous. Pretend you are confident even if you're not
• practise your presentation and time it	• swamp the audience with all you know – just highlight the main points.
• prepare a strong closing summary.	

Skills needed by those working in creative and media

For this part of the unit you will be required to complete three modules, one for each sector of the industry: visual arts, performance arts and media production. For each module you will create a media product. You might design a leaflet, be involved in a short performance or film an interview. Whatever it is you do, you will use all the skills we have talked about in this unit, from note taking to research, and from report writing to presentations, while at the same time practising particular skills in each area – be it performance skills, creative skills or production skills.

How to approach the modules

Before getting started first evaluate your current skills within the discipline and assess what skills you may need to learn or practise to successfully plan, develop and complete your creative and media product. This is a skills audit, and you may want to refer back to the section on this on page 17.

Job roles and career paths in the creative and media sector

As part of your modules, you will need to consider what job roles would be involved for your product to be made in the real world. The research for this should be done as you work through the unit. You need to remember that your school or college has probably supplied many resources for you to make your product that in the real world you would need to pay for or employ someone to do. You may also find that the way manpower resources actually work in the real world is different from your school experience. For instance where several people have worked on a product in school, in the real world it might only be one.

Creative and media job roles

If you have researched and prepared your products properly for the activity modules, you should already be well on the way to achieving this part of the unit and completing the research of job roles. You may have already discovered that job roles often overlap and it is difficult to pigeonhole people and jobs.

The multi-skilled nature of the creative and media workforce is reflected in this diploma's ethos of asking you to work across different disciplines and have transferable skills.

Creative work can only take place with the support of production, technical and administrative roles. Most media companies will have a creative team, a production and/or technical team and an administration department. However, depending on the size of the company, some staff may have to fulfil roles in more than one area. The majority of creative and media companies actually employ fewer than ten people, therefore an artistic director of a small theatre company may find they have to oversee human resources issues and finance for the company too. A reporter for a small radio or TV company might not only conduct interviews but also film or record them before returning to the studios to edit the material ready for broadcast.

FIGURE 1.11
Overlapping job roles in the creative and media sector

For assessment you will need to show evidence that you have researched job roles within the industry. Therefore for every module completed you need to go through the following steps and provide evidence of your investigation.

TRY THIS

Look at job descriptions and specifications that companies produce when they are recruiting. They are a very useful way to understand what the industry is looking for, as they will list the essential and desirable skills.

Step 1   Analyse the skills used in each module.

Step 2   Find out what job roles would be involved in the professional world to create the product.

Step 3   Find out what skills and qualifications the person fulfilling this job role would require.

Step 4   Find out what other professional roles this job role might work with and how their job roles relate to each other.

ASK

Many of the job roles you will research are advertised in trade and national press, where you can gather valuable information. Find some press adverts for the job roles you are researching. Some large companies will list the job descriptions and specifications on their website or you can ask for them by simply phoning the human resources contact. It won't cost the company anything to send you this information but it will be invaluable to you for your research.

LINKS

Use company websites to find human resources contacts and email them for any relevant job descriptions.

Ask your supervisor at your work experience placement to help you find out the following:

» What general skills does the company look for in new employees?

» How does the company carry out skills audits for new employees and monitor their needs throughout employment?

» What staff development does the company offer to its employees?

I want to be...

... an illustrator/animator

» What is your job title?

It depends on what job I happen to be doing! Author/illustrator/animation director/designer/art director/compositor/animator mostly!

» What creative and media products do you produce?

In the animation industry I create visual material for TV, web and film projects. My role and contribution changes depending on the project. I also write and illustrate children's picture books.

» As a freelance, how do you find work?

I have an agent who represents me as an author/illustrator and sets up meetings with different publishing companies, which, hopefully, result in me being offered work.

» What training have you had prior to working in the industry?

I did a Graphic Design degree at Hull (specialising in animation) and after that I did a two-year post-graduate course in animation direction at the National Film and Television School.

» What's the hardest thing about your job?

The instability. Not knowing if there is a job around the corner. You have to be extremely motivated and thick-skinned. The hard thing is juggling the short-term bread-and-butter jobs with more creative and long-term jobs and aspirations.

» What creative/technical skills do you need to be good at your job?

You have to be versatile and good at visualising things – translating the written word or an idea into moving images. You should have a solid understanding of what the various industry standard computer programs can do. You need a clear vision of what it is you are making but to be receptive to changes. Part of the creative process is to adapt and improve so it is important not to be precious and to take on board feedback.

» Where do you draw inspiration or ideas from?

In a commercial job, your brief will often include a visual reference, or an idea of style or tone that you should work towards. In self-generated work an idea can be inspired from anything, anywhere. I always carry around a notebook to jot down anything useful that I see or think of that might have the potential to be something.

» What is the biggest influence on your creative decisions during a job?

Time constraints and budget!

www.wonkybutton.com
www.hoonpatrol.co.uk

✱ Leigh Hodgkinson

Case Study

Disneyland Paris →

Originally called Euro Disney, the first Disney theme park in Europe opened on 12 April 1992 at a site very close to Paris, France. This location was selected over others in Britain, Italy and Spain mainly due to its central position within Western Europe, which means that over 68 million people are within a four-hour drive and 300 million within a two-hour flight radius.

During its early years the original park was beset by financial problems, which weren't helped by low attendance. However, in 1994 the park's name was changed to Disneyland Paris and by 1995 its fortunes had changed. In March 2002 a second theme park opened alongside the Magic Kingdom called the Walt Disney Studios. Today, the Disneyland Resort Paris welcomes over 12 million visitors a year.

Facilities
Disneyland Resort Paris covers over 600 hectares, and includes two theme parks (covering 76 hectares), the Disney Village and seven hotels, 59 attractions, five stages, 68 food outlets, innumerable shops, two convention centres, entertainment complexes and a golf course.

Personnel
Disneyland Resort Paris employees are all called Cast Members. They include reception, catering, beautifying (cleaning/gardening), protection and selling staff and all are encouraged to be focused on service to visitors. There are on average 12,200 Cast Members employed on short-term or permanent open-ended contract at any one time:

» representing 100 nationalities

» speaking 19 languages

» covering 500 professions

» with an average age of 33.

Over 1,000 artistes and creative professionals work at Disneyland Resort Paris (700 actors and dancers, 50 musicians, 150 creators, designers or decorators, 100 technicians and 30 seamstresses).

Behind the scenes there is also a team of creative people called 'imagineers'. It is their job to create the illusions and attractions throughout the parks, including the shows and parades, by experimenting with materials, designs and ideas.

Creating the 'magical experience'

Disney describe their visitors as 'guests', and everywhere that a guest might go is regarded being part of their 'magical experience'. Therefore every Cast Member that comes into contact with the guests will be performing in some way to help create and maintain that magic. All Cast Members are regarded as part of the team and teamwork is a core Disney value.

FIND OUT

Useful websites

www.disneylandparis.co.uk

www.disneylandparis-casting.com

Questions

» What personal skills do you think Cast Members need to carry out their role successfully? Which of these could be developed through the Creative and Media Diploma?

» What creative and media skills from which disciplines would be used to fulfil a creative role as an artiste or an imagineer?

» Consider the research skills required in planning a new attraction and/or parade. Can you identify key areas to research to fulfil the design brief?

» What different ways do themes parks and/or other tourist attractions use to attract visitors?

To be successful in this unit you will need to complete four modules. The three activity modules are in the visual arts, performance arts and media production. Each of these modules will include research and practical elements to produce the final product. They will involve producing evidence of your work, such as research reports, your Journal, class presentations and even blogs, as well as the final product. The fourth module is on your study skills and your ability to learn effectively. Your teacher will assess this module by observing how you work on the other three modules.

All your work must be presented in a Process Portfolio and could include finished work/product, ideas sheets and notes, your Journal, research work, documented trials and experiments, and planning documents.

Any performance work (process and final presentation) must be videoed by your teacher and a copy distributed to all those involved and be included in your Process Portfolio. Remember that at some point your video might be seen by examiners that don't know you, therefore make sure they know who you are on the video by taking a photo of yourself in costume or by introducing yourself to camera at the beginning of the performance.

To help you evaluate the process and remember all that you have done, it's a really good idea to keep a clear record of the progress of your creative work. With performance work this could be videoing rehearsals or run-throughs. An artist might take photos of their picture or sculpture as it develops, showing the different stages of production, different skills employed and the creative decisions. If your work is predominantly on a computer, why not keep older versions of the files you are working on, or take screen grabs of the processes you employ. This also helps you to see where and why you may have changed direction or approach to the creation of your product.

Finally, your teacher will assess and keep records of your progress for the learning skills module, a copy of which will be given to you to include within your Process Portfolio.

If you do not take these skills seriously, not only will your creative work suffer but you will run the risk of not achieving this unit.

TRY THIS

Research might be for the practical work or to find out about creative and media jobs.

REMEMBER

Your Process Portfolio should include all the documents that illustrate the creative process and the development of your ideas.

SUMMARY / SKILLS CHECK

» Applying skills to effective learning and thinking

You should know:

- ✓ how you prefer to learn so you can play to your strengths, while developing your weaknesses
- ✓ how to regularly carry out a skills audit to assess your strengths and weaknesses, so you can get further help and training
- ✓ how to keep a detailed Journal.

» Carrying out basic research in the creative and media sector

You should know how to:

- ✓ conduct and take part in a 'blue sky' meeting
- ✓ compile a brief for developing a creative idea
- ✓ reference properly to ensure you keep a record of all your resources. This is so you can support your decisions and avoid being accused of plagiarism
- ✓ effectively take notes – linear and pattern
- ✓ write for business, including reports, proposals and the Process Portfolio
- ✓ prepare and give presentations.

» Skills needed by those working in creative and media

You should:

- ✓ know how to use the creative and production process effectively
- ✓ complete modules within visual arts, performance arts and media production
- ✓ know how to analyse the skills required to fulfil certain roles.

» Job roles and career paths in the creative and media sector

You should know how:

- ✓ to research the job roles associated with the assessment modules
- ✓ to research the skills and qualifications a person would need to fulfil the job roles and how this person's career may progress
- ✓ different roles within the industry inter-relate.

OVERVIEW

We live in a world where all human-made objects around us will have passed through the hands of a visual artist. Everything, from the mobile phone in your pocket to the poster or TV commercial advertising it, from the humble egg box to the sculpture in your local park, has been *designed*.

Why is it that some computers, cars, mobile phones, just look so much better than others? We are probably influenced more than we realise by design. Good design will make you want to buy a painting from a gallery or a packet of breakfast cereal from the shelf in a supermarket. Design can transform lives, even choosing the right colour for the walls and the right paintings to hang in an office can enhance workers' lives and make them more productive.

The visual arts are not just about the long-suffering artist struggling to pay the rent and knocking out paintings that no one will appreciate until they are dead and gone. The visual arts are about a whole range of art forms created by artists, craftspeople, product designers, scenic artists, ceramicists, printmakers, photographers, fashion designers, textile designers, interior designers, graphic designers, illustrators and so many more. Some of these people will work for larger companies and organisations and some will operate as small businesses or as freelances, who work independently. These are all stimulating careers and can sometimes be very highly paid.

There has never been a time in history where the general public's awareness of what is good art and design has been so strong. It's time for you to find out whether you have what it takes to shape the material world you live in – welcome to the visual arts.

02

Visual Arts

Skills list

At the end of this unit you should:

» know about a visual arts form which combines two or more visual arts disciplines

» be able to plan the production of a visual arts product which combines two or more visual arts disciplines

» be able to create a visual arts product which combines two or more visual arts disciplines

» know how to monitor your own visual arts work.

Job watch

Job roles in the visual arts include:

» fine artist, printmaker, illustrator

» photographer

» ceramicist, jeweller, model-maker

» theatre/set designer

» furniture designer, interior designer

» graphic designer

» product designer

» fashion/textiles designer, costume designer, cutter

» gallery/museum curator

» arts administrator

» art educator.

Visual arts forms

During this unit your teachers will introduce you to a number of different visual arts forms, such as modelling with clay, drawing in pencil, making jewellery or prop making. Your visual arts product that you make for this unit has to combine two or more of the visual arts disciplines. Figure 2.1 summarises the main visual arts disciplines that you will learn about in this unit.

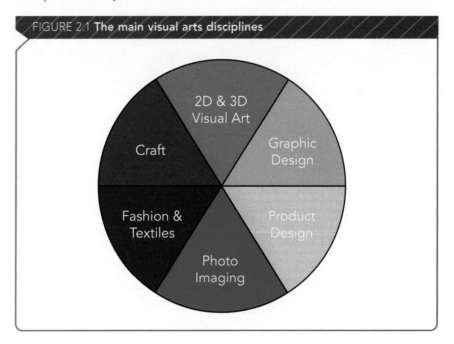

FIGURE 2.1 **The main visual arts disciplines**

The ability to combine different disciplines, techniques and skills is essential for the creation of any visual arts product. For example, David Rockwell, the set designer of the hit musical *Hairspray*, had to rely on 2D and 3D art skills in communicating his set designs to the director using sketches and a scale model of the set. He then had to have the understanding of paint effects and construction techniques to communicate effectively how his designs of a teenage girl's bedroom could be turned into reality by the senior carpenter and scenic artist.

Many companies need a team of artists to design, develop and create visual arts products across all the disciplines. Think about TV programmes such as the BBC's revival of *Dr Who*. The programme concept requires a creative team that makes the series itself, for instance the scriptwriters, costume and set designers and creators of the computer graphics. But in addition, the BBC also employs a completely separate creative group that designs and markets the merchandise sold as a result of *Dr Who*'s popularity. This includes a whole range of products, from remote-controlled Daleks to games that have been designed for the BBC website. These are all visual arts products that have been designed and created using visual arts skills.

Before we get started planning and making your visual arts product let's consider how visual arts forms are made, why they are made and who they are made for. Without this understanding your product will lack direction and focus, and you will find it harder to come up with an idea, develop it and consider whether it was successful.

How visual arts forms are made

To be successful in this unit, you are required to consider how a particular art form has developed over time. Your chosen art form might already have been decided for you by your teacher, however if the choice is left to you then you may need some help to select a suitable art form. In both instances you will have to consider the historical background of your chosen art form.

To help you do this we are going to consider some basics in the visual arts. These are ideas common to all disciplines about how art is created. An understanding of these ideas will help you to assess artwork, and decide for yourself why some are better than others. Let's start with some background on how to talk about art.

The language of art
Understanding a piece of visual art can be hard; deciding on whether it is better than anything else you have seen can be even harder. So how do we do this?

When we first look at a piece of work, whether it is a painting or a sculpture or a photograph, we first ask ourselves do we like it and then we ask ourselves, 'why?'. This is **analysis**, by asking 'why?' you are, in effect, analysing the piece of artwork. Answering the question 'why?' is essential if you want to be able to look at previous artists' and designers' work and decide what makes their products any good. Understanding how you feel about a piece of visual art will also help you assess others' work and improve your own.

We tend to do this instinctively. I'm sure you've all looked at a piece of art and said or thought to yourself that you like or dislike it because of the shapes/colours/subject matter, or whatever. For this diploma, and as you carry on studying or working in creative and media, you will need to record these thoughts more formally, perhaps writing about them and certainly talking about them. To do this professionally, you will eventually need to know about what we term the 'formal elements' of art, which are part of the language of art. There are many formal elements, here are a few to think about.

TABLE 2.1 Formal elements in the visual arts

Line	Shape and Form	Colour	Pattern	Texture
The use of line. This includes: • its *weight* – heavy or light, thick or thin • which direction it goes in • where it leads you/takes your eye • what perspective it uses. Line also defines the outside edge of all art and design *Paul Klee (1879–1940) an artist and master draftsman, used line drawings that grew out of fantasy or dream imagery. He described his technique in these drawings as 'taking a line for a walk'.*	Shape helps us to recognise the object, person or animal, or determine whether the image is abstract. Form is shape that takes up space, like objects in a painting or a sculpture on the landscape. Shape can be seen as flat and form as not. However don't get this confused with it actually physically being 2D or 3D, as a painting can still have form. *Henry Moore (1898–1986) a sculptor, used shape very effectively. In his huge bronze 'Family Group', 1950, for example, even though there are no distinct faces with eyes and noses we still recognise the shapes as being human.*	Artists and designers use colour in many ways, for instance to: • express emotion • evoke a mood • create a reaction • attract. Designers have moulded our expectations in the way colour is used in our everyday lives. For example, we always expect fire engines to be red and police cars to have blue flashing lights. Colour association plays a huge part in our lives. *Francis Bacon (1909–1992) a painter, used a lot of red in his work, which could be interpreted as symbolising the bloodshed of war.* *Pablo Picasso (1881–1973) a painter, famously had a 'blue period' when this colour dominated his work.* *The Fauves, an art movement, used bright colours in an unrealistic way on purpose to shock.*	Pattern is the way in which lines and colours are used. It can be used to describe the repetition of shapes in any piece of art or design. Some artists use specific patterns to create optical illusions in their artwork, known as '**op art**'. *Bridget Riley (b1931) an op artist, is influenced by* **pointillism***, a method of building up a picture using dots as used by the artist Georges Seurat.* *Laurence Llewellyn-Bowen, interior designer and presenter of the TV programme* Changing Rooms*, uses pattern in wallpaper to create a particular feel to a space, making it seem larger or smaller!*	Texture is about surfaces, which we appreciate through touch and sight. Texture is an important element in fabric, collage, relief work, paintings and sculpture. In the world of film and special effects, creating the texture of an animal's fur and skin is a real art. *Rick Baker, make-up artist, six-times winner of an Academy Award for best make-up on films such as* An American Werewolf in London, *and Rob Legato, a CG expert who has worked on the computer generated visual effects creating animals in the Harry Potter films, have perfected two different ways of using texture to add reality to the creatures they create.*

FIGURE 2.2 **Henry Moore's sculptural forms are unmistakably human**

As you look at art products, past and present, think about using this language to describe and analyse them. We have only focused on five elements here, but you will find other words to help you think about a piece of artwork. As you walk around a gallery or discuss artwork with others, you might consider elements such as: tone, space, rhythm, scale, and overall composition – that is the arrangement of all the elements in the work. And don't forget subject matter – ask yourself the question: what is the artist trying to communicate? A story? An idea? An emotion?

Skills and techniques

Many skills overlap between disciplines, and the skills from some disciplines are needed to successfully complete work in others. This is why you are being asked to combine more than one discipline in the creation of your visual arts product. Take fashion designers, how can they design fabulous collections for their next fashion show without 2D skills to sketch their ideas? Think about product design, you would find it hard to be a product designer without graphic design and drafting skills.

So it won't be difficult for you to cover at least two disciplines in the making of your visual arts product, however you must consider how others have made similar products and how the skills and techniques have changed over time.

For example, if you are planning to make a mask for use in theatre, you will need to describe the similarities and differences between examples of mask making past and present, considering the developments that have taken place. This can be in the materials or the techniques used to make them. You will have plenty to talk about just by thinking about cultural changes, developments of technology and the availability of materials over time. Remember, though, this is not just about research, you also need to practise any new skills and techniques you acquire and demonstrate these skills in you final product.

Why visual arts forms are made

To fully understand the product you are making and the style and techniques you will be using during the creative process, it will help you to understand its origins: why was it made in the first place and how has it developed over time? This knowledge will help you to understand how others have made creative decisions in the past and you will find it easier to come up with ideas yourself and develop them further.

Suppose you had to design a new mobile phone. Because it is such a familiar object you might assume you would know straight away what is wanted from a mobile phone and get stuck in to designing straight away. However, a professional would never assume anything, they would always do their research. This research starts in the past, considering the origin of mobile phones, why they were developed, how they have changed over time and why. Then they would look at the present. What are the similarities and differences between products, what's good about them, what isn't? What's your competition? What are the latest trends to take into account? What do people want from their phones today – chances are this is not the same as it was even five years ago. There are hundreds of designs to look at, all different shapes, sizes, functions, designs and colours. Also don't be swayed too much by your own personal preferences. Your favourite phone is not necessarily someone else's – a good designer is objective. So, in short, even if a product has an obvious function, you need to look a bit deeper to consider why it exists and analyse what is best about the current designs.

THINK

In your class think about your mobile phones and/or mp3 players. Discuss among yourselves:

Why do they exist?

Are they essential items?

Don't simply settle for the straightforward answer! A mobile phone is not just for phoning people and an mp3 player is not just for listening to music? Or is it?

Think about why you all have different designs and/or makes of the same product. Are these reasons that you as a designer could use to create an even better product?

Compare the features of all the phones owned by people in your group. Draw up a table in Word or Excel for the phones and their features. See if you can rank them in terms of things such as value for money, functionality, fashion, compactness, etc.

LINKS

Craft or art?

For hundreds of thousands of years, people have developed skills and crafts for entirely practical purposes. Think of things such as pottery, glassmaking and weaving. If we take weaving as an example we can consider useful objects made using weaving skills and techniques, such as baskets to carry things before we had plastic bags and fences to keep the animals in the field before we had barbed wire. These craft skills are still used today for their original practical purposes, but they have also developed into art forms. They can be used to create objects of beauty with no practical function at all. Think about the amazing sculpture 'Willow Man' by Serena de la Hey next to the M5 motorway. Although it has been made using the traditional craft techniques of basket weaving and fence making, it has no practical purpose – it is there simply to be looked at and enjoyed.

FIGURE 2.3 **Serena de la Hey's 'Willow Man' combines traditional craft techniques and fine-art 3D disciplines**

Serena's sculpture is an excellent example of how complicated it can sometimes be to understand why a piece of art is made. The table below summarises reasons why visual art exists and why visual artists create the art in three different areas.

TABLE 2.2 **Art in different areas**

Commercial Art	Craft	Fine Art
Artist understands market needs and desires. Artist makes something to fulfil a given brief. Commercial pressures of resources, costs and potential sales influence every part of the creative process.	Artist understands a specific need for a handmade traditional product. In making something that serves a purpose the craftsperson will try to ensure it is individual to themselves. This can make the product relatively expensive.	Artist creates the work to fulfil own desires and creative goals. Idea is the key. The art can change the world and how people think.

These are quite sweeping statements that you and your teacher may or may not agree with. But this is the point. It is very difficult to make general statements about the visual arts. For example, under which heading would you place a fashion designer? Well, depending on the designer they could be placed under any of them. Fine artists are often **commissioned** to produce works of art. Serena de la Hey would have been commissioned to create 'Willow Man', so does this mean that she is a commercial artist? This is a discussion that could fill the rest of the book and therefore it seems sensible to merely be aware of these issues, as it gives you the ability to discuss and consider why art has been created, both past and present.

So, when considering your chosen art form, try to work out why it was originally made and why people would want it now. This is what the next section discusses, who are you making it for?

THINK

Think of any human-made item in your house. What Table 2.2 heading would you put it under?

Do you think the artist/designer made creative decisions about it purely for commercial reasons, or did they want to bring some of their own artistic individuality to it? Do you have any art in your house that is simply there to look at? What do you feel about the artwork? Does it serve a purpose for you? For instance does it set a mood, or do its colours match the room?

Take a photograph of your chosen item and stick it in your Journal with notes on your thoughts about it. Alternatively, write your notes and use a digital copy of your photograph in a word-processed document.

LINKS

Who visual arts forms are made for

Visual art is created for all number of reasons as previously discussed. Fine art is often created to communicate an idea, to make you think and change your opinion on larger issues. Craftspeople will produce beautiful handmade items that you can use as well as enjoy looking at. Commercial designers will produce functional items that are stylish. Companies will commission visual art to promote or advertise their products.

You need to think about the differences between these types of visual arts product and, more importantly, what category your final product falls into and who you are making it for. It is absolutely fine for you to create a piece of visual art that is to be hung on a wall in a gallery where it will provoke an emotion from the audience that looks at it. It is also just as suitable for you to design and make something completely commercial that you want to sell. At some point, however, you need to consider who is the audience for your product.

FIGURE 2.4 **This piece of jewellery by designer Michelle Watling is a piece of art designed to be both decorative and to be worn**

The largest percentage of artwork produced around the world is not, in fact, to hang on a wall but to serve a purpose dictated by its potential audience. You therefore need to know enough about your audience to ensure your product is successful. Here are a few questions to get you thinking.

» Age range

Who usually consumes your product? If it's something for the car then it's a pretty safe bet that it will be someone aged over 18. However, you can narrow you audience down further – a car owner, for instance could be an 18-year-old or someone in their 80s. Will your product appeal to both, or will it be much more narrowly targeted? A state-of-the-art in-car sound system, for instance, might be aimed at the younger end of the market.

» Affordability

How much would your audience usually be prepared to pay for the product you are making? Do your research, go to a department store and see what the prices are for a range of your type of product. Don't forget to compare the quality of the product and its design with the price. If you are looking at kettles, for example, the least expensive is likely to be cheaply made, one colour and very boring to look at. The most expensive will have extra features, such as being cordless, be made from stylish materials, and have a more attractive appearance.

» Style of product

Good design doesn't come cheap, but people will pay for it. Take the iPod, for example, there are much cheaper mp3 players on the market, but there is something about the style and design of the iPod that makes it desirable enough for people pay the extra few pounds for it. The iPod has really become a fashion accessory, a sort of style must-have.

FIGURE 2.5: The iPod has become a style icon due to its design

Planning the production of a visual arts product

The visual art that you create must combine two or more disciplines from the art and design sector. Why not look at Figure 2.1 again to remind yourself about the main visual arts disciplines. In this section we will look at the processes you need to go through to come up with your ideas, develop them and plan how you are going to make your product. We will also look at how you should manage the whole process from planning to creating the final product.

Depending on the assignment that you are set by your teacher, you may find that it is very clear from the start which two disciplines you will learn about and use to complete this unit. You may be constrained by the facilities and expertise available to you at your centre. However, in some cases you may have some flexibility, for example, the group may learn about 2D art but be given some scope in choosing what other discipline they will use alongside it.

Whatever your situation, and your teacher will make sure this is clear, you must ensure that your work in the Process Portfolio for this unit clearly demonstrates that you have researched, planned and created a visual arts product using two different disciplines.

Journal

To complete this learning objective successfully you must produce evidence of your planning. Most visual artists would normally record their planning in a sketchbook. It is often the process of recording the planning that helps or inspires the development of ideas for the final product. Do regard the term sketchbook in this unit as being the same thing as your Journal.

What is a sketchbook?

For artists, designers and craftspeople, using a sketchbook to plan and record the creative process is vital. The sketchbook in itself can be used as a creative tool to reach the final outcome. It is a visual map that records the journey you have travelled in order to reach your destination, in other words a visual diary. It is a personal record of your thoughts and ideas; it is evidence of the stages and processes you have planned and carried out; it is your way to review and evaluate your work. Your sketchbook should include all the work you do in coming up with your ideas: research, analysis, development, experimentation and planning.

Here are four top tips to help you make the very best of your sketchbook.

1. It should show all your workings, no matter how sketchy.

2. It must be personal to you! If you include other people's ideas as inspiration or reference, that's fine, but make sure you give them a credit.

3. It must show a wide selection of work.

4. Annotating your work is extremely important. You may have got a fantastic idea from a particular artist but just showing or referring to their work is not enough, you must explain how it has informed your work and ideas.

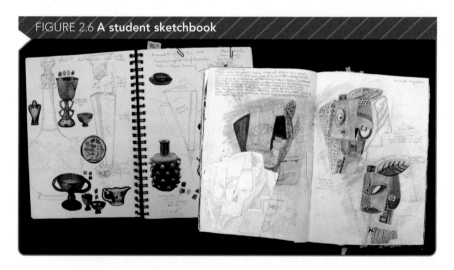
FIGURE 2.6 **A student sketchbook**

Responding to a brief

So how do artists and designers get started? Artists often receive what is called a commission, where a gallery, organisation or individual will ask them for a particular piece of work, which will be agreed upon by both parties for a set fee. This often applies only to well-known artists who have a reputation for a particular type of work, as in the case of portrait photographer Annie Leibovitz and her recent stunning portrait of the Queen. Your teacher might 'commission' the piece of work you will produce by giving you a brief to follow.

Designers, such as set designers, will often be employed on the strength of their previous work. Freelances move from job to job for different clients, building up their reputations as they go along.

Some companies and commercial organisations will have visual artists in-house, such as Marks & Spencer or MFI, who employ creative teams to design their collections.

If you work for a company you will still be set a brief but you will be working much more as part of a team and you are generally salaried. That means at the end of each month you will be paid, rather than receive a set fee like a freelance.

Whether you have been set a brief within a team or whether you are working on a commission on your own, the processes you go through will be the same: research, analyse, experiment/develop ideas and plan the production. You will face the same constraints, too. Time and money are the main ones, both of which have an uncanny knack of running out if you don't plan properly! You will probably face constraints of time and availability of resources in your project for this unit. You must be aware of these and plan for them accordingly.

Coming up with your idea

If your teacher has given you a brief, then you have a starting point to base your initial research on. If you haven't been given a specific brief, then you will have to generate your own ideas.

Whichever the case, it's a good idea to start with a concept map. Let your imagination wander and write down all the ideas that come to you, no matter how strange or stupid some of them might seem at first – it's a bit like brain storming for just one person. Make visual connections between your ideas on your map. Look back at Unit 1 for more about concept maps. You might prefer to record your first ideas in written form, or as a collage of images or hand-drawn sketches. Try to note down every idea or connection you think of, no matter how small.

Preliminary research
If you are finding it difficult to come up with ideas at this stage, you should consider doing some preliminary research first. There are lots of sources you can use, which are listed over the page.

Research sources:

» the Internet

» newspapers and magazines

» books

» television programmes and films

» music

» observations – including your own sketches and photographs.

You should gather all the information together, be it downloads and pictures collected from the Internet; doodles; sketches from observation or from secondary or primary sources; pictures from newspapers/magazines; photographs, past or present, that show your ideas – these could be your own or borrowed from someone else; photocopies and information from books or even physical objects, such as bus tickets or a piece of packaging.

You can do more research to narrow down your shortlisted ideas, or to develop your final idea.

Considering work from the past and the present

It is important that you can show your understanding of the context of your product by looking at its history and background. This information can be collated from books, the Internet, museums or galleries. You therefore may need to visit museums or galleries as part of this process.

You should try to show understanding of the work of others in your planning. How do these practitioners convey meaning and feelings with their work? You can illustrate your findings with your own drawings or collages using materials such as pencil, charcoal, crayon, pastel or paint. You might even want to make small models if the work is 3D.

When looking at others' work, think about how their methods and approaches might affect the way you carry out your own work. You can compare and contrast using written information or illustrations. In your analysis you need to say why you have chosen these particular examples and show how they relate to your own ideas.

REMEMBER

If you use other people's material, be it photographs or information from books, magazines or the Internet, you *must* reference it, and credit it if you use it in your final product.

JOURNAL TIPS

Include in your sketchbook postcards, or even the entrance tickets, to remind you of your gallery or museum visits. Jot down your feelings about certain exhibitions or individual pieces of work and make quick sketches of them, or of particular features that interest you.

Planning and doing – production schedules

In the commercial world there is always a time constraint in the production process, whether it's a theatre production, publishing a book or creating a website for a client. The process starts with the brief being set or the commission being made and a date for completion agreed. In order to ensure the final product is created on time and to budget, a production schedule is drawn up that outlines what has to be done, by whom and when. Usually, the creative team will meet in a series of production meetings to keep everyone up to date with progress and identify any problems.

The client controls the timescale in which the product is completed. In your case, your teacher will tell you when your work must be done by. As in the real world, you should keep your teacher (client) informed of progress, significant changes and any problems that might mean you are unable to complete the project on time.

An interesting exception to the rule in completing a commission in the timescale dictated by the client is the Sagrada De Familia church designed by Antonio Gaudi in Barcelona. This must be one of the longest-running works on a commissioned piece of art ever known. It was started in 1882 and still isn't finished! Gaudi died in 1926 but work still continues and it is estimated that it could take another ten years to complete. But don't follow this example – you must ensure that you deliver your product on time to your 'client' that is, your teacher!

Planning your own schedule

Whether you are working alone or in a group to complete your visual arts product you will need to plan your time and resources. Think about all the processes you need to go through. Do you need to book a studio, or time on a computer, or firing time in a kiln? Before you start, with the help of your teacher draw up a list of the stages you will require, estimate the time you need for each and list all the resources. If you have to book out equipment, such as cameras and microphones, build that into your schedule. You will then be able to see at a glance what you need and when. Check your progress against your schedule regularly so that you can see if you are falling behind, or if you need to make more time anywhere, change any deadlines or keep your teacher informed of any issues or problems. Make a note of any changes, problems or developments in your sketchbook.

JOURNAL TIPS

Make sure that significant changes to the production schedule are recorded and the reason documented in your sketchbook, or separately in you Process Portfolio.

DID YOU KNOW?

Deadlines for fine art are often self-imposed by the artist, unless they are working on a commission. This means that a piece of fine art can take years to complete! Unfortunately you won't have this luxury!

REMEMBER

How well you plan your schedule will have a direct effect on the smooth running and successful completion of your work.

Materials and processes

You will probably have to try out a number of different techniques or ideas before you decide on your final approach. You need to show examples of the different materials or techniques you have experimented with. For instance, you may wish to try out different painting techniques or make models or **maquettes**, which you can photograph and put in your sketchbook. Include fabric samples and swatches, and record any experiments you do to try out ideas, such as burning, melting, **trapping** or machine embroidery.

Don't forget to make notes on colours – include colour samples, look at different paints and dyes, and experiment with surface textures. Look at the list below and maybe try some out in your sketchbook. Keep larger samples and experiments in your Process Portfolio.

As appropriate, try different techniques, such as:

» painting: watercolour, oil, acrylic

» collage

» drawing: pencil, pastels, charcoal, chalk

» batik

» printing: screenprinting, lino printing, etching

» sculpture: wax, metal, wire, plaster or clay.

The list is endless!

Choosing a material that is suitable for the final piece is vital. It would be no use having a headdress that flopped in the performers' faces all the time so they couldn't see where they were going, or a vase made of a porous clay that lets the water out!

Look at techniques and treatments and record what skills you need to be able to carry out your final piece using them. Graphic artists may start with pen drawings before moving to the computer and using sophisticated image manipulation tools. A sculptor will almost always make smaller carvings or models of the final piece before starting the real thing. Using wax blocks or plaster to experiment with is a lot cheaper and faster and means you are able to iron out all the mistakes before you start the final piece.

REMEMBER

You must ensure that you have evidence of using two different disciplines during the creative process. For example, preliminary drawings before starting work on the computer will involve both 2D and graphic-design skills, so make sure this evidence goes in your Process Portfolio.

A set designer will always build a scale model of the final design; this will often be out of card and painted by hand. It will be given to the scenic artist to use as a reference when he or she is making the scenery. If you are painting or decorating scenery it is important to produce samples of colours/textures and any effects that are required. One of the issues you will come up against with scenery is how fireproof it needs to be; you cannot stick things that are liable to go up in flames all over a piece of scenery. It is important that you do your research very carefully in this area. There is more on the health and safety aspects of your work later in this unit.

REFLECT

During the process you must continually reflect on and record what you are doing. For example, think about:

✱ What materials are you using and why?

✱ Have you shown development?

✱ What has changed since you first started?

✱ Have you made changes for the better? If so, how?

✱ What problems have you encountered? Have you solved them? If so, how?

Creating your own visual arts product

You have come up with your idea, researched it, chosen your materials and drawn up a production schedule. Now all you have to do is make your product!

But before you dive in make sure that you are absolutely clear what is required and that you have read the brief thoroughly. For example, if you are making a costume or headdress for a specific person do you need to measure them? Success or failure could ride on this – you can't have a costume that is too big or a headdress that will fall off if the person moves around too much! If you are designing graphics for a website check that they are appropriate for the age group your are targeting. Check and double-check who your audience or end user is, and make sure you design and make your product to suit.

Try and think of all the practical aspects of your task. For instance, if you are mounting an exhibition have you measured the space properly, have you tried out your ideas in rough first? But most importantly, remember to take advice – and always ask for help if you need it.

Experimenting, changing and developing ideas

Experimenting is crucial for deciding on the final design and ensuring the success of the final product. You may find you will try out your ideas on a smaller scale before attempting the final piece, experimenting with all the different materials to make sure, for example, that the paint will work on top of a particular type of paper, that the material is the right texture when it is applied to the mask, or that the glaze you have mixed for your pottery is the right colour once it has been fired. All three of these products could have been a disaster, and have wasted valuable time and money, if you had gone straight into making your final product without experimenting first.

Through experimentation you may find you have to change large parts of your initial design. Suppose, for instance, you are making a headdress for a show. You have been taught about ceramics and have decided to use a glazed ceramic face-mask as the basis of the headdress, but through experimentation you realise a ceramic mask is going to be too heavy and you can't fix the decoration you want to use to it. You might at this stage revise your plans and use papier maché instead.

There is always a danger in this part of the process to go too much the other way and to keep on experimenting and changing your ideas, the result being that you don't leave enough time to complete the task. But there will come a point when you will need to commit your self to making the end product.

Even when you have got to this stage, you need to understand that ideas may still have to be modified and developed, right up to the last minute. The key to this is to remain flexible. Suppose you have designed a new leaflet to advertise a local club. Through experimentation you have designed a page layout for the leaflet that incorporates a couple of photos, however as you are finishing your design you find that the photos simply don't fit the composition of the leaflet and you require something different. Although separately these photos looked fantastic, you have to make the decision that they don't work for the overall product and you need to source more suitable ones.

Sometimes you have to revise your plans because of things completely beyond your control. Suppose at the last minute the person who is going to wear your headdress goes off sick before the show and the replacement has a larger head; this is where you have to show the utmost professionalism and work quickly to adapt your work.

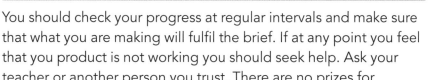

JOURNAL TIPS

Record in your sketchbook all the decisions you make, for instance, how and why you have made changes or developed your idea in a different direction. You could photograph or film the various production stages.

Are you achieving your purpose?

You should check your progress at regular intervals and make sure that what you are making will fulfil the brief. If at any point you feel that you product is not working you should seek help. Ask your teacher or another person you trust. There are no prizes for struggling with something that is not working. It may be that you do not have the technical knowledge to be able to continue, but with some expert help you can solve the problem and move on. Never be afraid to ask for help.

Safe working

Working safely is really important for everyone and in your Journal you should reflect on what you did to improve the safety of your working practices.

Things to consider when working with different media/tools:

» Wear appropriate clothing that allows you to move around freely.

» Be careful with wearing jewellery, it might get caught in machinery.

» Be aware of the safety procedures of any substances or equipment that you use, such as solvents, blowtorches and electrical tools.

» If in doubt ASK.

Things to consider for technical production work:

» Be careful lifting heavy equipment or large pieces of set and furniture. Always make sure you have enough people to help you.

» Make sure electrical equipment you are using is PAT tested. There should be a sticker on the plug of every piece of equipment to tell you whether it's been tested within the last 12 months.

» Don't use ladders without proper supervision. There are strict rules about working at heights, if in doubt ask a member of staff.

» Do not stand on chairs or tables to carry out technical work.

» Every production should have a risk assessment and every educational centre will have examples on how to do this.

For further information on current legislation and handouts, visit the Health and Safety Executive website at www.hse.gov.uk

Monitoring your own visual arts work

If you have been working hard to maintain a detailed and comprehensive sketchbook, then you shouldn't find it hard to complete this section of the unit. Don't forget that your sketchbook can include writing and should definitely include reflections on your work as it progresses. For instance:

» How well did your plan go?

» What did you need to change and why?

» What worked well and what did not as you experimented?

» How well did you succeed in achieving your intentions?

» What did others say about your work?

It's really important that you understand how to review your progress and react to your findings to improve. No one gets everything right first time in the creative arts; success requires you

REMEMBER

You could do a skills audit or carry out a 360-degree feedback on your work within this unit and on the final artwork.

to experiment and try out various options until you are happy you have the right solution. Whatever happens, at some point you must review the process and make decisions to improve it or do things differently in the future.

REFLECT

What do people think? It might be terrifying to find out but it's crucial for your development. Remember, some of the most valuable people to receive feedback from are your teachers and fellow students!

Show your work to others whenever you can. If possible, try getting reactions from different age groups.

You might find it interesting to ask people for feedback before they know what the brief is, than ask them again after they have seen the brief. Did they think you met the brief? Did their overall opinion of your work change?

It's no good getting feedback if you don't listen effectively. Write down people's comments as soon as possible so that you will remember what they said. You could take notes during the discussion or even, with their permission, record your conversation. If you don't remember or understand their comments, ask them again.

LINKS

Here are some questions you might ask yourself in your evaluation.

» Did you complete each task to the best of your abilities?

» The next time you create a piece of art and design work, would you do anything differently?

» How were you at

   – keeping on schedule and meeting deadlines

   – keeping a detailed sketchbook

   – exploring and developing ideas

   – using different art media?

Hopefully, if you have thought carefully about your product and followed the advice given in this unit, you will have a successful outcome. Remember, it is just as valid in your evaluation to explain what went right and how you ensured success, as it is to look at your problems or mistakes.

At any work placement you will be surrounded by visual arts products – either made or used by the business you are working for. Ask your work experience supervisor to help you answer the following:

» Does the company produce or sell any products or services that involve the visual arts? If so, what disciplines would they come under?

» Which staff working for the company need specific visual arts skills?

» What visual arts products or services are used by the business? For example: a graphic design company to design publicity materials.

I want to be...

... a jewellery designer

» What creative and media products do you make?

I work on my own to design and make mixed-media, haute couture, contemporary jewellery, commercial cast-silver jewellery, wedding jewellery, headdresses and tiaras.

» How do you get and distribute your work?

I have to liaise with clients for commissions and with gallery owners to stock my products.

» Do you have to regularly show your work to others during the creative process?

I have to monitor my own work and carry out quality control. If the item is a commission then I will show the client design ideas, but apart from that they would not usually see the work until it is finished.

» What's the hardest thing about your job?

Finding my clients and marketing my work.

» What creative skills do you need to be a good jewellery designer?

Design skills – taking an idea from an initial source and developing it to make a wearable object. Keen observation skills, creative thinking, technical drawing skills to convey an idea to the client, marketing and display skills.

» When developing creative work, where do you draw inspiration or ideas from?

My primary inspiration is from nature: plants, seeds and vegetation. I also enjoy learning new techniques and the challenge of introducing them into my work.

» What do you most enjoy about your job?

Creating ideas and the challenge of problem solving.

» What is the biggest influence on your creative and development decisions?

From the creative perspective – to make something beautiful to hold and wear. From the development perspective – to make a high-quality product that fulfils it purpose. For example, easy to wear, fastens easily, has the wow factor, etc.

» What equipment do you use in jewellery making?

Basic equipment includes: workbench, blow torch for soldering, safety mats, files, barrel polisher, pickling acid, hydraulic press to make shapes, pliers, saw, snips and hammers.

www.katemichelle.co.uk

Michelle Watling

Site Visit

Venture – New Generation Portraits →

Venture is a **franchise** of portrait photographers that has redefined the look and style of portrait photography. Founded by the current CEO and award-winning photographer Brian Glover-Smith, the first Venture photography studio opened in 2000 and the company rapidly became a global leader. Venture now has nearly 100 studios across the UK as well as a growing number in Ireland, Hong Kong and the USA.

Every Venture tells a story

In a revolt against stiff, lifeless and posed portraits, Venture's products, services and 'experience' capture their core target audience of families and children in a fun, exciting and original way. The aim is to show the clients as themselves through the notion of storytelling. Venture is also innovative in its presentation of the finished photographs using montages, prints on canvas and digital effects.

Facilities

Each Venture studio has a gallery, studio and viewing area. The light, bright studio is equipped with state-of-the-art digital equipment. Photos are sent digitally to a central office for a technician to prepare for viewing. This includes minor retouching and adjustments to composition, colour and contrast. The photographs are viewed by the clients in the viewing room first as a slide show to music, then individually in the different sizes and layouts the clients can buy.

Personnel

Venture employs the following personnel at the studios and at its central office:

» Style Director – head of photography at a studio, responsible for quality and style

» Appointment Co-ordinator – telephone and face-to-face consumer relations

» Venture At-Home Consultant – visits clients at home, promoting the brand and selling the product

» Digital Artist – digital manipulation, artistic retouching and preparing images for print

» Exhibitions Representative – promotes the brand and represents Venture at exhibitions and in retail outlets.

Each studio also employs a general manager, photographer, receptionist, studio sales manager and often a trainee photographer.

Trainee photographers experience all aspects of Venture studio work to help them develop skills and to progress to Photographer. Trainees need a professional qualification at HND or degree level. Photoshop and IT skills and a good portfolio as well as drive, enthusiasm and ambition are also required.

Questions

Visit some portrait photography websites, including Venture's, www.thisisventure.co.uk, and consider the following questions:

» What specific visual arts skills do you think someone needs to take a successful photo?

» Are there any other skills that a good photographer should have and why?

» What makes a successful photograph? And what makes it not?

» What visual elements are used to create a Venture product?

» What techniques on visual artwork or photography can you learn from Venture?

Assessment Tips

To complete this unit you will need to create a piece of visual art combining more than one visual arts discipline. Through evidence in your Process Portfolio you will need to demonstrate that you know about visual arts forms that combine one or more disciplines and that you have considered how your chosen product has developed over time.

You must present a Process Portfolio that includes the following.

» Research into visual arts products that combines more than one discipline – this can be presented in many different ways, for example as a written document or an oral presentation. Whatever form it takes it should include:

– similarities or differences between visual arts products that combine more than one discipline

– uses and purposes of the visual arts products

– audiences the visual arts products were created for.

» All your ideas and evidence of explorations of the ideas for your final visual arts product.

» Your production plan – including any revisions and changes, with reasons for those changes.

» Your Journal – a traditional sketchbook for this particular unit.

» Finished visual arts product. This could be in the form of photographs, video or a computer disk, depending on the product.

You will also be provided with observation records by your teacher to include in your Process Portfolio.

Although you will only produce one final piece of work that combines more than one visual arts discipline, it is important that you demonstrate that you have been introduced to a number of visual arts products by your teacher and that you have documented this research, before choosing one to turn into your final piece.

REMEMBER

Your professionalism during the production process is key to successful completion of the unit. Not only will good attendance, punctuality and attitude allow you the time to focus on your work effectively, but your ability to turn up on time can be included in your assessment by your teacher.

SUMMARY / SKILLS CHECK

» Visual arts forms

You should know:

- ✓ how visual arts forms/products are made, what skills and techniques are required to create them
- ✓ the visual elements that have shaped art and design past and present
- ✓ why visual arts forms/products are made
- ✓ about the audiences for different types of art and how they affect the production and process of creating it
- ✓ about the purpose of the art; is it to meet the needs of the audience or the creative mind of the artist?

» Planning the production of a visual arts product

You should know:

- ✓ how to use a sketchbook (Journal) to record the development of your ideas
- ✓ how to research, analyse, develop and experiment with ideas
- ✓ the value of a production schedule
- ✓ about the materials and processes involved in creating your art.

» Creating your own visual arts product

You should know:

- ✓ how to experiment with ideas
- ✓ how to change and develop ideas
- ✓ whether you are achieving your original purpose for the production and meeting the intentions of the brief
- ✓ how to work safely.

OVERVIEW

The performance arts include music, drama and dance. Although these three disciplines are very different, they are closely linked – there is scarcely a performance arts event that doesn't combine at least two of the three. How could the ballet survive without music and drama? How could actors tell a story in a musical without dance and music? Would your favourite pop singer be as exciting without the theatricals of their performance and the choreographed dance routines?

It's easy to watch actors in movies and decide that you are going to concentrate purely on your acting skills to be as good as them. However this is a highly competitive industry, and to give yourself the best chance of getting work you should become as skilled as possible in as many different areas as you can. Even if you only ever act, none of the other training will be lost. Dance skills, for instance, will ensure you can move well; singing will help with voice projection; and any musical training will help with timing. If you look at some of the great names in acting today, serious actors, such as Dame Judy Dench, Ewan McGregor and Al Pacino, your will find that they have all done their fair share of training in other disciplines and have all relied on their singing and dancing skills to further their careers.

As well as acting, music and dance, in this unit we will also look at all the non-performance job roles within the performing arts. These underpin all performance art productions. Without technicians, designers, writers, costume designers and make-up artists, to name but a few, there could be no live performance. You will combine your performance and behind-the-scenes skills in rehearsing, performing and evaluating a live production.

This unit will help you learn to be critical of you own performances and those of others, and will require you to see as many types of shows and live performances as possible. It will provide the perfect opportunity for you to explore all areas of the performance arts, find out what areas you are good at, and evaluate where you need to improve to be employable in the future.

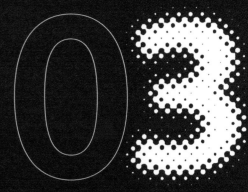

Performance Arts

Skills list

At the end of this unit you should:

» know about performance arts

» be able to take part in preparations for a live performance

» be able to take part in a live performance

» know how to monitor your performance work.

Performance arts

To be successful in this unit you will need to plan and prepare a performance piece and perform it in front of an audience. You cannot start this process without fully understanding what your options and opportunities are within the performing arts. We will start by looking at the types of performance companies that exist in the UK, where performances are held and what types of audiences are attracted to performance art.

THINK

Think about the following questions. Write down your thoughts and compare them with your group. Did you all come up with the same things? Add any additional ideas from your group's lists to your lists and keep in your Process Portfolio.

✳ What types of performance companies are there?

✳ What types of shows can you think of?

✳ What types of venues are there for performance arts?

✳ What do you think audiences of live performances want to see?

LINKS

Think of a way to record your findings in Word. Consider tables, lists, columns. Can you show who had which ideas?

Once you have worked through the Think activity, it should provide you with enough understanding to quickly make informed decisions about the kind of performance work your group would like to put on and how to make it happen. The following sections will give you some more detail on the sort of performance art and companies that exist in the UK.

Theatre and dance companies

There is a diverse range of theatre and dance companies in this country, from major companies run by hundreds of full-time staff based at a particular theatre to small companies based in a home office relying on **freelance** expertise as and when required. As theatre and dance companies tend to be very similar in the way they are run we will consider them together.

There are two main types of theatre or dance companies:

» production companies

» producing theatres.

Production companies

Production companies vary in size but are generally run by a small team of permanent staff. They don't have a permanent venue and when they start preparing for a show they will then employ a team of freelances to fulfil creative, performance and technical roles. They will hire theatres/venues or share the ticket income with the theatre they are using. If the production company has a good reputation they can actually demand a fee from a theatre, rather than having to hire it. The companies run productions to make a profit and will usually have financial backers/investors to **underwrite** the shows. These are known in the business as '**angels**'.

An example of a small professional theatre company is Jam Theatre Co. (www.jamtheatre.co.uk) based in Marlow, Buckinghamshire. The company currently has just two full-time members of staff; the artistic director and a producer. However, in the space of a year they will employ anything between 50–100 freelance or part-time practitioners. They also hire workshop and rehearsal rooms when required.

Larger production companies will have a large permanent administration staff, but they will still employ everyone for their individual shows on a freelance or short-term contract. This includes West End producer Bill Kenwright's operation (www.kenwright.com). Kenwright started life in the industry as an actor but then went on to produce musicals such as Willy Russell's

FIGURE 3.1 **A professional West End performance brings together the skills of hundreds of people, from performers to producers**

Blood Brothers and more recently *Cabaret*, as well as being responsible for record-breaking UK tours of *Joseph and the Amazing Technicolor Dreamcoat* and *Blood Brothers*.

Cameron Mackintosh (www.cameronmackintosh.com) is probably the UK's most prolific producer ever with hundreds of shows in the West End, Broadway and around the world. Shows include *Cats*, *The Phantom of the Opera*, *Les Miserables*, *Miss Saigon* and *Avenue Q*. Again, all the staff for the individual shows will be employed on short contracts only for the life of that show.

Rambert Dance Company (www.rambert.org.uk) has a permanent building, which includes dance studios, offices and some technical workshop space, but no performance space – they have to find venues to perform at. It has a large permanent team that includes a music director, rehearsal director, a management team for the 20+ full-time dancers, administrators, technical staff including lighting, sound and costume, marketing and press officers, and an audience development and education department. They are currently funded by the Arts Council.

Other production dance companies include Richard Alston, resident at The Place in London (www.theplace.org.uk); and Matthew Bourne's New Adventures (www.new-adventures.net), resident at the Sadler's Wells Theatre in London. This is a contemporary dance company that has had international success with productions such as *Edward Scissorhands* and the all male *Swan Lake*.

Some production companies may work on only one or two productions, or seasons of productions, a year. Although there are some differences between dance and theatre companies, the largest companies of both types aim to develop a production that can be put on a West End stage or can tour in the UK and/or internationally for as long as possible. The longer run a show can sustain the more money it makes for investors and producers!

ASK

Research some of the companies listed above in more detail. Can you go and see one of their productions? Do they have DVDs of their shows? Can you talk to someone at the company and ask them how they go about their business? For instance, how they choose their productions and venues and recruit their staff.

Producing theatres

A producing theatre is one that creates productions mainly for its own venue, although sometimes, if they are successful productions, they may tour or even transfer to larger theatres, for example in the West End. Producing theatres will typically have a large, permanent, full-time staff, not only because they have to run the building, but also because they must produce new material so that there is always a production running at the theatre. Most of the work is created by the theatre, although they may sometimes take productions from other companies.

Producing theatres are very expensive to keep running, and although they are committed to selling tickets and making a profit, they usually get a lot of money or grants from local councils and the Arts Council. They will run productions for a fixed period of time, often four weeks, or operate a **repertoire** system (see below).

Types of producing theatre

There are three types of producing theatre:

>> repertory

>> repertoire

>> stagione.

Repertory theatres are usually regional theatres, such as the Watford Palace Theatre (www.watfordpalace.co.uk), that stage a season of plays one after another. Production runs typically last 2–4 weeks, and as soon as one production has opened the next show will go into rehearsal.

Repertoire theatres house big national companies, such as the Royal Shakespeare Company in Stratford (www.rsc.org.uk). They

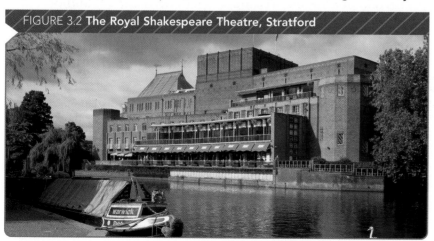

FIGURE 3.2 **The Royal Shakespeare Theatre, Stratford**

rehearse a number of plays for any given season. Throughout the season each will perform for a few nights before switching to another.

Stagione are similar to repertoire theatres having a season of just a small number of productions, but these alternate to allow at least one night off between each performance of each production. Theatres will keep productions in their repertoire for many years and re-rehearse them for each season. This kind of programming is especially important to attract international stars to perform in opera or ballet so that they can rest their voices between shows. The Royal Opera House (www.royalopera.org), is an excellent example of a stagione producing theatre.

ASK

Research the National Theatre, studying the programming of their theatres. What kind of theatre is the National? Can you find out everything you need just from the website?

www.nationaltheatre.org.uk.

Compare the ease of use of this website with that of another theatre. Try and find the answers to the same questions. Which site was better?

LINKS

Bands, ensembles and orchestras

Most musicians in the UK are essentially freelance, only a very few are fortunate enough to have full-time jobs with music organisations, such as orchestras. Some jobs are not permanent, but they are long-term, such as working in an orchestra on a large-scale musical in the West End, which could last from a few months to many years. Before we consider the different types of musical groups and performers it is important to consider a group of people that create work within the music industry – promoters.

Promoters

Promoters are individuals and/or companies that book artistes to play at venues and promote (publicise and organise ticket sales) the show. Some promoters are employed by record labels to publicise their bands and to book tours, others will develop their own shows in a very similar manner to a theatre company, employing musicians or ensembles to perform in one-off or long-running shows.

Two examples of very successful promoters are Raymond Gubbay (www.raymondgubbay.co.uk) and Serious Music

DID YOU KNOW?

Deutsch Entertainment AG has now bought 75 per cent of Raymond Gubbay, but the UK branding is unlikely to change.

(www.serious.org.uk). Both companies have a small administrative team to run the company and will employ the technicians and performers specifically for individual shows or events.

Orchestras

Orchestras, such the London Symphony Orchestra, employ musicians on a full-time basis, adding extra freelance musicians if and when needed for different types of music. Orchestras usually have a home in a concert venue and produce a season of performances of different music. They are often financially supported by the Arts Council or other funding bodies.

The London Symphony Orchestra (www.lso.co.uk) is resident at the Barbican Centre in London where it performs most of its London concerts. It has a large pool of players to call on for its concerts. It is supported by the Arts Council and the City of London.

There are excellent regional orchestras too, such as the City of Birmingham Symphony Orchestra and the Northern Chamber Orchestra (www.norch.co.uk).

Bands

Many bands get started and rehearse on an **amateur** or semi-professional basis. Members often need to do other work to support themselves. They rehearse and play gigs in pubs and clubs in their spare time, building a fan base and hopefully releasing recordings through independent record shops and the Internet.

Only bands that manage to get a record deal can usually afford the luxury of working full-time with their band, producing albums and performing around the country or internationally. A record deal usually provides band members with an **advance** given to them to produce the next album. Sometimes they might get a weekly salary. But be warned, the million-pound record contract does not mean the band gets paid that amount. The mansion will have to wait! The million pounds is usually a commitment from the record label to invest in your band – a lot of it gets eaten up by legal fees and administration, and a lot of this investment will be recouped by the record label once you start selling albums before you see your share of the profits.

Individual artistes

Being a professional musician, dancer or actor means you have to find work for yourself. Actors and dancers will usually have an

DID YOU KNOW?

Many bands will use small promoters to get them tours. One of the most popular touring platforms to build up your fan base is the student union bar!

agent to help get them work, while musicians typically manage themselves. There are also such things as diary services for the really busy professional musician, and people called 'fixers' that book individual musicians for gigs.

See if you can find out more about diary services and fixers. What do they actually do?

Consider using the industry press, the Internet and phoning people to get the information you need.

Create a Word file and write a short description of each, explaining what they do.

Performance art shows

There are many different types of shows that are regularly put on in theatres and other venues around the country, here are just a few: plays, reviews, operas, comedy shows, musicals, cabaret evenings, classical ballets, rock concerts, contemporary dance shows.

What makes the above shows different from each other? Ask yourself the following questions about each of the different types, this will help you to see whether you have the skills, facilities and equipment to consider staging each type of performance.

* How many people does it require?

* What disciplines and skills are required by the performers?

* What staging is required?

* What are the technical requirements, e.g. lighting/sound/set?

* What costume and make-up is required?

Summarise your findings in a table created in Word or other suitable program.

Performance venues

So far we have looked at the different types of companies that exist in the performing arts sector and you have considered various different types of show. It is now important you know what venues are available and how the staging within these venues can affect the suitability of the venue for the show you are creating. You'd be surprised what impact the venue can have on the type of show you decide upon and how to produce and stage it.

Presenting theatres or receiving houses

The majority of theatres do not produce their own shows, instead they take productions that have been rehearsed, built and performed at other similar venues or by a production company. These theatres are called presenting theatres or receiving houses. Most West End theatres and regional theatres around the UK are receiving houses.

Concert venues

Concert venues are run in a very similar way to theatres. Sometimes they are old theatres, or other large buildings converted from a previous usage, sometimes they are purpose-built to host concerts. Purpose-built auditoriums are usually designed carefully with the **acoustics** in mind so that orchestras can perform without amplification and without the sound balance becoming distorted. The Symphony Hall, Birmingham (www.thsh.co.uk) is a good example of a purpose-built concert venue.

Street theatre

Possibly the cheapest venue you can get, as long as you get permission, street theatre dates back to medieval times. Actors, dancers and musicians perform in the streets and marketplaces of towns and cities. Some venues, such as Covent Garden in London, are well known for their street entertainers. The Shrewsbury International Street Theatre Festival (www.shrewsburystreetfest. co.uk) is a great place to see proper street theatre. Street theatre is arguably not as common as it once was, with busking musicians being the most common street performers seen today.

Types of stage

What makes a venue suitable for a show? How can you set up your venue to fit the type or style of performance art you are producing? Knowing the different ways you could present and stage your work will really help you to come up with an interesting show.

Its very easy to assume that your audience will be sat in rows in front of you but, depending on the type of performance you are planning, this might not be the best way to engage your audience. Here are some ways of staging a show that you could consider.

» Arena – the audience sits in raked seats around one side of a circular stage area.

» Thrust – typical of Tudor times this staging gives the audience a view of the stage from two thirds of a circular building.

» Proscenium arch – traditional theatre staging with a raised stage with wings and a curtain. The audience sits in raked seats in front of the stage.

» Theatre in the round – the audience surrounds the space where the action takes place. Sometimes the stage is raised, but not always. This allows for a very intimate performance.

» Traverse – an intimate rectangular staging with settings for scenes at either end.

» Promenade – the audience moves around the space with the players (promenade means to walk) and usually becomes part of the action surrounding them. Promenade performances can take place in large outdoor spaces, such as parks or gardens.

Who is your audience?

As part of your Process Portfolio you will need to discuss who your audience is. This is crucial for you to be successful, not only on a creative level but in business. There is no point in spending weeks, months or even years developing a show if you do not have a clear vision of who it is actually for.

Venues that sell tickets will have a very clear idea of who goes to see what shows; they will have box office computers that keep records and mailing lists of their audiences, with their contact details and what they have been to see before. Box office and marketing departments can then mailshot their audiences with future shows they might be interested in. They can also see how far someone is prepared to travel to their theatre to see a show, and compare this with local competition. This helps them decide on programming, for instance whether it is worth them having a show that has already visited a theatre 60 miles away.

Unfortunately your school or college is unlikely to have this kind of facility, although as part of your course you may decide to try and set up a system that records your audience data, especially if you run many shows throughout the year. You could try asking your local theatre's marketing department if they could send you any general information, such as percentages of tickets sales for different types of shows. But remember, they will not be able to tell you any confidential information about individual customers.

TEAMWORK

Audience research

So how can you find out about who goes to see what in your local area? The best way is to conduct primary research yourself – ask people! This research will really help your understanding of what people want to see.

In a group carry out a survey local to your centre. The aim of the survey is to collect information about what audiences want to see. As a team compile your questions and undertake the survey. Decide among yourselves who will do which task. When deciding on your questions remember the following:

✱ Keep the questions and the survey short and simple to understand.

✱ Be clear about what you are asking.

✱ Avoid questions that influence the answers.

✱ Use multiple choice, or 'Yes or No' answers, don't use open questions.

Decide where you are going to conduct your survey – maybe your town centre, or outside your local cinema or theatre at the end of a performance.

Make sure you ask an appropriate cross-section of the local community – don't simply ask your friends at school or college!

Your questions should help you find out whether people go to live performances, and if so, what type. You should also find out what you can about your interviewees – think about their age, whether they are male or female, whether they are local, and so on.

Try your questions out on fellow students first, to make sure that they make sense and are easy and quick to answer.

Discuss your results among the group. What do they tell you? How will they affect your decisions about your own performance?

Create your questionnaire on the computer and print out a sufficient number for your survey.

Using the computer to create a master copy means you will all use the exact same questions.

LINKS

Preparations for a live performance

The performances you will be involved in must combine two performance-related disciplines, for instance a piece of drama with elements of music and/or dance. Remember, some in the group may take on responsibilities behind the scenes.

Before you start you must assess the skills you have in the three disciplines – Drama, Music and Dance. You can then identify any areas you need to work on in order to be able to successfully put on your live performances.

As well as the performance roles you also need to consider the administrative, production and technical jobs that go on behind the scenes. You may find that you would prefer these sorts of jobs to performing on stage. In any case, it is very important for performers to understand how all the job roles that go into making a production interlink so that everyone works well as a team to create, plan and present a performance. Any good actor, dancer or musician should know enough about sound, lighting and staging to understand how it affects them and enhances a live performance.

TRY THIS

Always be open to new job roles – the more you understand about the whole process of putting on a performance, the better performer you will be.

Journal

Throughout the pre-production, production and performance make sure you keep your Journal up to date. It will support and provide evidence for your learning. Include in it:

» reflections on your work

» decisions taken and reasons for taking them

» changes to plans and reasons for making the changes.

Part of your assessment is on your ability to reflect on your work and change what you are doing and how you are doing it. You must therefore think about:

» how well you plan your work

» what you need to change and why

» what works well and what does not in your experiments

» how well you succeed in achieving your intentions

» what others say about your work.

To help you with thinking of things to write about in your Journal, you will find some helpful boxes in the margins on the following pages that give you some things to think about.

JOURNAL TIPS

If you regularly reflect on your work and record this in your Journal you will find writing you evaluation at the end of the whole process much easier.

TEAMWORK

As this is a collaborative project try to set up a WIKI – an online space that enables collaboration, communication and the sharing of information. There are many websites available where you can set up pages to be a kind of on-line log or Journal that all invited guests can edit and add to. But remember that your final Process Portfolio must still have clear evidence of your own individual work, so only use this as a communication tool, not as your Journal.

Think about the security aspects of your Wiki. Who is allowed access – how will you manage this?

L I N K S

Workshop ideas

Now you have researched all the possibilities of how performance arts are presented and looked at the skills you have within the group, it's time to come up with ideas on what you are going to produce. Depending on how your teacher has designed the assignment you may have some constraints on what you can do. These need to be established straight away so that your ideas can work within them. For example, you might not have a choice of venue, but you can decide on how to set the stage and seating in the space you have been given.

Ideas storm

You saw how to undertake an ideas storm in Unit 1. This is the perfect application for this technique. It's a good idea to have an ideas storm to decide on the theme and type or style of your production.

Theme

You may already have a strong idea of what you want the theme of your production to be. If you haven't there are all sorts of areas you can look to for inspiration, for instance personal experiences, hobbies, history and newspaper headlines. When you have decided on your theme you need to ask yourselves the following questions:

» Will it engage an audience – make them laugh, make them cry?

» Does it have a strong narrative or idea?

» Is the whole group committed to the concept?

» Is there enough scope/material to devise a performance piece that incorporates two or three disciplines?

Format and style

Once you have your theme, you need to think about the different ways you could present it and the performance styles or techniques you could include. The production, for instance, might take the form of a dance, musical, play, review or pantomime, and devices you could include might be audience participation, use of a narrator or mime.

Research

Once you have decided on your theme and format, you will probably have to do some research. Here's a reminder of where you might go to find information:

» libraries and museums

» your parents, teachers, other students

» poetry books and drama scripts

» paintings and photographs

» newspapers, magazines and books

» cinema, CDs and DVDs.

JOURNAL TIPS

Don't forget to write up all of this in your Journal. Make sure you include your feelings and any decisions or ideas you contributed too.

JOIN IN

A great way to develop your ideas and start to create material for a script is to use improvisation. Assume the characters in the scene and decide how the scene should start and how it should finish. Then try improvising in character. It probably won't be great to start with and will take time to develop improvisational skills, however, if you find you like how an improvisation went and what a character said – write it down! It's good for everyone in the group to join in with this activity, even if they are not all going to be in the performance. It's always good to practise improvisation skills and it will ensure that everyone is involved in the creative development of the piece.

LINKS

The key to good improvisation is listening to what the other actors are saying so you can respond appropriately and keep the scene moving.

Technical roles

It's time to define your roles and responsibilities within the production. Even if some of you are going to specifically concentrate on only performance or technical roles, it is likely that you will all have some responsibilities for finding props, costumes, painting the set or setting up for the performance.

A professional production company will have a creative team that answers to the director.

FIGURE 3.3 **The creative team structure**

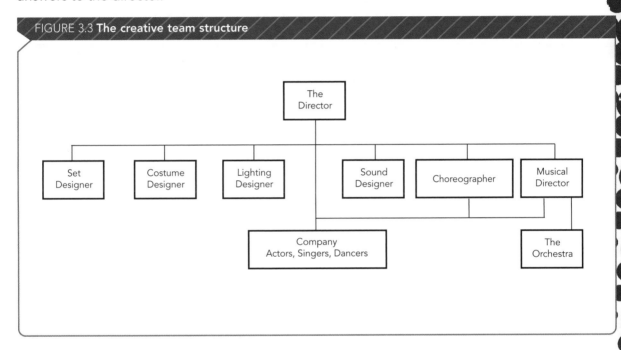

Your teachers may take on the roles of director, choreographer and musical director, but you as a company will need to assume some of the other creative roles to make sure everything gets done.

MANAGE

There is a lot to do in putting on a production. One person cannot do everything. Keep notes on how your teacher/director manages the process. What techniques do they use? Do they delegate different tasks to different people? How does everyone communicate? Do you have progress meetings to check everything is going smoothly? How do they deal with any problems that crop up? Reflect on the management process – what went well, what could have been done better, and keep the notes in your Journal or Process Portfolio.

Think about how you will manage your own work. Can you set up blank schedules or progress sheets in Word as templates you can then use for various different tasks?

There are also technical roles that have very important functions during the planning, rehearsing and performance of the show. Not all of these roles, even in a professional theatre company, can have specific people employed to do them. So often, for example, actors may have to take on stage management responsibilities. If this happens they are called Actor ASMs (Actor Assistant Stage Managers).

Let's look at a basic list of technical departments and the job roles within them that you may need to share out to ensure your production runs smoothly.

TABLE 3.1 Technical and production roles

Stage Management	Lighting or LX Department	Sound Department	Wardrobe/Costume Department	Workshop
SM – Stage Manager	Lighting Designer	Sound Designer	Costume Designer	Set Designer
DSM – Deputy Stage Manager	Chief LX	Sound Engineer	Wardrobe Supervisor	Carpenters
ASMs – Assistant Stage Managers	Lighting Operator	Sound Assistant	Dressers	Scenic Artists
Rehearsals Stage managing department is responsible for propping – buying, hiring or making props, setting up the rehearsal room and supporting the Director.	**Rehearsals** The Lighting Designer decides what lighting is needed to help tell the story. This can be simply light to make sure that performers can be seen, or adding colour and other lighting effects, to set a time, place or mood.	**Rehearsals** The Sound Designer decides what sound effects or amplification are needed to help tell the story. Edits sound effects or recorded music on a computer to make sure it fits the performance.	Assistants **Rehearsals** The Costume Designer decides on appropriate clothes for the performers in consultation with the Director. Making, buying or hiring costumes.	**Rehearsals** The Set Designer in consultation with the Director designs the staging and any set, furniture to be hired or bought and how it should be dressed. The Carpenters will make anything for the set and the Scenic Artists will paint the set.
Performances Stage management department is in charge of the stage and the safety of performers. Carries out scene changes. In large shows the Stage Manager may 'call the show', i.e. tell the technical operators when to carry out lighting and sound cues.	Rigging all the lights ready for technical and dress rehearsals. **Performances** Lighting Operator works the lighting desk as decided by the LX Designer and Director.	**Performances** Sound Engineer and Assistant operate audio equipment to ensure that sound effects are played at the correct time and that any amplification is balanced correctly.	**Performances** Wardrobe Supervisor ensures costumes are looked after and that the Dressers and Assistants help performers with costume changes.	**Performances** These roles do not usually have anything to do during the performances. However they could take on Stage Management tasks as they will have an understanding of the set and how it works.

Although you can take on a technical or production role to support the performance you must make sure that your research and work is always within the context of the development of the performance and not spend all your time on a computer editing sounds or up a ladder moving lights around. You have to take a full part in the process of developing an idea, planning, rehearsing and developing the show and then supporting the actual performance.

Production schedule

The creative process for putting on a show, from the original idea, through planning and rehearsing, to preparations for performance in front of an audience, is called the production process, so the show is 'in production'. The production process needs to be carefully scheduled and monitored to ensure everything that needs to happen does happen, on time and preferably to budget.

With the deadline for a performance weeks if not months away it's very easy for early rehearsals and meetings to be unfocused. It is therefore vital to devise a detailed production schedule that will give you clear milestones you have to achieve on a weekly basis – there is always something that needs to be completed sooner than you think, and if you don't get something done in time it can have a serious impact on your progress through the project. When taking on a big task that might go on for several days or even weeks, it's a good idea to break it down into smaller chunks, which you spread out over the allocated time. If you don't do this, the tendency is to think you have plenty of time and leave everything until the last minute. This will either mean that your work will be rushed and not of a high standard or you won't hit the deadline.

FIGURE 3.4 A professional production schedule.

Date	Rehearsals	Stage Management	Lighting	Sound	Wardrobe / Costume	Workshop
3 - Feb - 08 4 - Feb - 08 5 - Feb - 08 6 - Feb - 08 7 - Feb - 08	Read-through	Collate Stand in Props			Research Period	Design Set
10 - Feb - 08 11 - Feb - 08 12 - Feb - 08 13 - Feb - 08 14 - Feb - 08	Rehearsals	Prepare rehearsal room Rehearsals	Research available equipment, budget for hire Preliminary design	Prepare sound effects & music	Make/source costumes	Build
17 - Feb - 08 18 - Feb - 08 19 - Feb - 08 20 - Feb - 08 21 - Feb - 08						
24 - Feb - 08 25 - Feb - 08 26 - Feb - 08 27 - Feb - 08 28 - Feb - 08	Run-through Rehearsals Technical	Attend Run-through	Attend Run-through LX fit-up	Attend Run-through Sound fittings	Attend Run-through Costume fittings Alter/change costumes	Build set on stage Paint floor Technical
3 - March - 08 4 - March - 08 5 - March - 08 6 - March - 08	Dress 1 Dress 2 Peformance 1 Peformance 2					Dress 1 Dress 2 Performance 1 Performance 2

Some things depend on other things being completed before they can be done, and if these slide it can have a serious impact on the progress of the group. Whatever responsibilities you have in the production, you must stick to your schedule.

Production meetings and planning

It's a very good idea to hold regular production meetings to check on the schedule and how it is progressing, identify any problems and see everything is running smoothly. Make sure that deadlines are realistic and that you have the skills and/or resources to fulfil the task. It's better not to promise something than to be unrealistic. Once you have decided on your **milestones**, then stick to them.

Stage time

During the later stages of rehearsals think about 'stage time' – that is who has access to the stage and when. You will find that lots of people other than the cast will want to work on the stage: to paint the set, rig up lighting and sound equipment and so on. The person taking on the stage-management role needs to negotiate with everyone to ensure all have time to complete their tasks. If you are scheduled to have stage time, don't waste it, be punctual, have everything you need with you and get on with the job.

Rehearsals

The rehearsal period for a show is just as important as the performances. This is when you practise all your skills. Here are some golden rules to help you get the most out of the process.

1. Be PUNCTUAL and aim for full ATTENDANCE – this way you will benefit from all the time given and not let yourself or your group down. Just one missing person at rehearsal can make the whole session a waste of valuable time.

2. Bring your SCRIPT if you have one, and a PENCIL and NOTEBOOK. When the Director starts putting moves in you need to write down where you are supposed to go or stand to help you remember. The Director may give you notes about your character or advice on how to play the scene. Record this so you can work on the script on your own.

3. LISTEN to the Director and to the other actors you are performing with, not to the people waiting to start work. The more you listen the more you will learn. When you are not in a

scene still pay attention to what is going on – if you get involved in other conversations you will lose your concentration and focus, and you may miss something important.

4. Use your IMAGINATION as you are working and think of what your character might do. Offer these ideas to the Director but be prepared to ACCEPT that they might not be used. The Director has the ultimate authority and is the one person with an overall picture of the whole performance.

5. Keep up your ENERGY and STAMINA – rehearsals can sometimes be long and laborious. Things often have to be repeated over and over again in order to get them absolutely right. You need to put all your energy into each rehearsal so that the Director can get a proper idea of what things will look like.

6. Be a good GROUP MEMBER – help where you can. Go over someone's lines with them if they are having trouble – offer to set up at the beginning and clear up at the end.

7. Don't forget to ENJOY the process – this will boost the energy level of the rest of the group and the time will fly by.

8. Rehearsals can be boring at times, especially if you are not needed for a scene. You can learn a lot from watching what is going on, but sometimes you will have time on your hands. Have your JOURNAL with you so you can use the time usefully in making notes about what you have just rehearsed, your thoughts or any other observations.

FIGURE 3.5 **Full participation in rehearsals is essential if you are going to give a professional performance**

The most useful thing to remember when you are acting is to keep it real and think about what the words are actually saying. Try the following exercise with a friend and notice all the changes you make both physically and vocally.

Character A and Character B find themselves sitting in a railway station. They are old friends and are waiting for someone to arrive on the last train. There is no one else around. Each character has only one line of dialogue and they must say it in as many different ways as they can.

Character A: I can't wait any longer.

Character B: Please don't go.

Try to keep this going for about three minutes – using pauses, physical changes and emotional changes. Stop and then discuss how this felt and what sort of artistic decisions you made e.g. who was the someone? What did they want? What was your attitude to the characters?

Safe working

Working safely is really important for everyone and you should reflect in your Journal on what you did to improve the safety of the production.

Things to consider for performers:

» Wear appropriate clothing, including footwear, that allows you to dance, move, act, play your instrument correctly, etc.

» Be careful about wearing jewellery, as it might get caught or pulled during physical movement in scenes, especially when you are trying out ideas.

» Behave professionally and appreciate that you need to be able to trust each other. Some improvisation or physical work can be dangerous if you are not all concentrating and looking after each other's safety.

Things to consider for production technical work:

» Be careful lifting heavy equipment or large pieces of set and furniture. Always make sure you have enough people to help you.

» Make sure all electrical equipment you are using is PAT tested. There should be a sticker on the plug of every piece of equipment to tell you whether it's been tested within the last 12 months.

» Don't use ladders without proper supervision. There are strict rules about how high you can go up a ladder. If you are under 18 you should not work at heights over one metre. If in doubt ask a member of staff. Do not stand on chairs or tables to carry out technical work.

» Every production should have a risk assessment and every educational centre will have examples on how to do this.

REFLECT

Ask to see the risk assessment that will be done on your production. Do you think it covers all the health and safety issues adequately? If not, why not? Is it too restrictive? Give your reasons.

Write a short report as if to the person who did the risk assessment, saying what you think is good and where there are any problems or things that haven't been covered.

L I N K S

For further information on current legislation and handouts, visit the Health and Safety Executive website at www.hse.gov.uk.

Taking part in a live performance

The day arrives and all your hard work has finally come together for the performance. Everything should be in place.

Are you ready?

Are you ready to perform? Have you hit all your deadlines or milestones? Being ready for the performance is not just about learning your lines in time, remembering your steps or the notes in a piece of music. Your role is only a small part of the total performance. Stop and consider whether your production is truly ready for an audience. Remember, the more prepared you are the less likely something will go wrong and the less you need to be nervous.

Equipment and resources

Make sure all the equipment is working well before the start of the performance so you have time to get something mended or replaced if there is a problem. It is common practice for the lighting technicians to switch on all the lanterns at 10–15 per cent (meaning that the faders operating the lights are at this level). This both gently warms up the lamps in the lights so that they are less likely to blow when you start flashing them or changing lighting scenes quickly and gives you an opportunity to check whether any lamps have actually blown.

Sound engineers will always carry out quick sound checks to ensure that all their CDs and microphones are working. If you are using radio mics always make sure you are using a fresh battery for every performance.

Props and costume

If you are not careful props and costumes will go missing. Be disciplined and set up props tables and clothes rails with clear labelling. Make a list of all the props that should be on the table for the beginning of the show. If you are doing several performances, then get into the habit of resetting the props and costumes straight after the show or scene in which they are used.

FIGURE 3.6 **Organising your props and costume carefully back stage will help the performance go smoothly... so not like this!**

This way, if a prop or costume has gone missing or is broken, you will notice it instantly and have time before the next performance to find it or replace it. You don't want your lead actor to be running around five minutes before the performance starts because they can't find their costume or an important prop!

Warm ups

As part of study in the three disciplines you will have learnt about the importance of warming up your body properly. Proper warm ups before you perform are important to make sure the cast is ready, focused and working as a team. It's not unusual in small companies to see the technical staff also taking part in warm ups.

TEAMWORK

Try these warm ups for concentration and energy before your performance.

Warm up for concentration:

The whole group stands in a big circle and holds hands with their eyes shut. The object is to be able – as a group – to count up to ten with only one person speaking at the same time. You all need to really listen and focus – someone will start with 'one' and then someone will follow with 'two', etc. If two people speak together you all have to start at the beginning again.

Warm up for energy:

The whole group stands in a big circle holding hands. They crouch down on their haunches and everyone repeats the word 'energy' – very softly at first but building up the volume. As you get louder and louder start to stand up until all your hands are in the air and you are all shouting 'ENERGY!'

Safety

It is crucial that you set up your staging and seating safely. Some pieces of set can be very heavy and if not secured properly they could hurt someone and ruin your performance. Any raised areas of staging must be marked with tape so that both performers and audience can see where the edge is. If the height of staging approaches one metre then it should have handrails.

REMEMBER

Make sure all fire exits are clearly marked and clear of hazards.

The performance

If you have worked hard during the planning and rehearsal process then you should be able to enjoy the performance. People usually become nervous because of a lack of preparation and the uncertainty of whether everything is going to be all right on the night! However, a little nervousness is a good thing. If you are well prepared you should be fine and any nervous energy will be positive.

What makes a good performance?

The key to a good performance and getting the best grades is whether you manage to communicate your intentions to the audience. There are two levels to this, the first is whether the group communicated the intentions of the performance work. Did you make your audience feel how you wanted them to? Did they understand the story or what you were trying to say? The second is whether you communicated your intentions for the character you were playing. For instance, if you were playing an old person but your audience did not recognise this, then you did not communicate effectively.

Communicating to you audience is not just saying the lines right or playing the correct notes on your instrument, it takes a concentrated performance where you remain in role at all times. Fluency of lines, dance moves or musical performance is only the start – you can be technically perfect but still not make audience contact. However, technical competence will make you feel more comfortable so you can concentrate on your character or the emotion you want to convey to your audience. Think about whether you are making eye contact with the audience and if you are physically moving as the person should be, or are you looking at the floor or standing nervously fiddling with you costume and mumbling your lines.

You also need to be responsive to the other performers and technical team. If anything goes wrong, for example if a cue is missed, work with the other performers and stage crew to keep the performance flowing.

If you communicate and respond effectively with your team and the audience with fluency, imagination, energy and commitment then you will be successful within the assessment of this unit.

Monitoring and evaluating your work

Keeping a detailed Journal as suggested at the beginning of this unit will get you half way to completing what you need to prove for this part of the assessment. You should be able to reflect on the following questions:

» How well did you succeed in achieving your intentions?

» What did you need to change and why?

» What worked well and what did not?

» How well do you feel you did?

» What did others say about your work?

Don't forget, you could do a skills audit or carry out a 360-degree feedback on your work within this unit and the final performance.

It's really important that you understand how to review your progress and react to your findings so as to improve. No one gets everything right first time in the creative arts; you will experience a lot of trial and error. What is far more important is the ability to review your work and make decisions to improve it or do things differently in the future.

How were you at:

» meeting deadlines

» suggesting ideas on characterisation and movement

» practising and developing your skills

» keeping focused and concentrated during rehearsals?

Ask yourself:

» Did you complete each task to the best of your abilities?

» The next time you perform, what would you do differently?

Why not ask your audience what they thought. You could ask them to fill in a concise questionnaire or speak to them at the end. If you are performing to other students from your centre, then maybe you could have a discussion afterwards and get feedback.

Fully document your thoughts and say how you would change things in the future to improve the show or your own performance.

Create a table in Word or Excel giving some do's and don'ts guidance from your own experience of putting on a performance.

LINKS

Ask your supervisor at your work experience placement to help you answer the following questions:

» Does the company ever organise promotional events?

» What staff would take on the responsibility of organising such events?

» What skills would they require?

» What performance skills are valuable within the company and for which specific job roles?

I want to be...

...a performer

» What is your current job?

I am a performer in shows at Legoland, I perform in the stunt show as a character, and we also have puppet shows, where I retell fairy stories using puppets.

» Do you work in a team? If so, who else do you work with?

There is a team of performers and a technical crew. For each performance of a puppet show there are two puppeteers, one technician and one narrator. For the stunt show there are six stunt performers and one narrator, one technician and one stage manager.

» At what stage in the creative process do you get involved?

I become involved when rehearsals start, although I have no input in the script writing and concept. During the rehearsal period the performers help with the development and evolution of the show. The director largely tells us what he/she requires but will sometimes ask for our input.

» Do you have to regularly show your work to others during the creative process?

When we are rehearsing, we perform the show to the creative director, and then the bosses from Legoland come to see it to check they are happy with it. Once the show is up and running we have

clean up rehearsals and the director comes in to check on the show.

» What's the hardest thing about your job?

When it is pouring with rain or snowing and there are only a few people watching, making sure you still give as much energy to every performance. Sometimes we do up to eight shows a day.

» What creative or technical skills do you need to be a good performer?

You need to have passion and enthusiasm for what you are doing and a good vocal technique.

» What is the biggest influence on your creative decisions and the development of your product during the creative process?

The director and the creator of the shows. What the boss says, we do!

» What do you most enjoy/like about your job?

I love the children and that it makes their day to come and see our shows. I love performing and I work in a great team.

www.legoland.co.uk

Vikki Sparkes

Case Study

Watford Palace Theatre has been producing shows and plays for over a hundred years. Its Grade II listed Edwardian theatre first opened in 1908 as a music hall. It is now the only producing theatre in the region and it attracts over 100,000 visitors each year.

In 2002, the theatre was awarded lottery funding of £8.8 million to pay for much-needed refurbishment which has created more public space for audiences, new seating, lifts to all levels, an extension to the stage area and scenic docks, superior technical facilities and accommodation.

The Watford Palace produces nine shows a year, rehearsing for four weeks and running performances for up to three weeks. It strives to support and develop new writing, and has enjoyed a national reputation with many productions transferring to the West End or UK tours, such as David Farr's *Elton John's Glasses*, and Simon Gray's *The Late Middle Classes*, which won the 1999 TMA Award for Best New Play.

The theatre's programming has a wide appeal, from modern plays to adaptations of classics, comedies to traditional pantomimes. Watford Palace also hosts one-off performances and touring productions programmed around its own in-house productions.

Facilities

After refurbishment the theatre now includes two bars, a daytime café, a new box office, and much larger public spaces than are typical of an old Edwardian theatre for audiences to enjoy during intervals. This has been achieved by expansion into an adjoining building, allowing a much more comfortable and enjoyable experience for audiences while retaining the charm and beauty of the original theatre.

Expansion of the building footprint also allowed for a deeper stage with a crossover, a full-height fly tower, scene dock, six dressing rooms with showers and toilets, a well-equipped wardrobe department with laundry, and improved lighting and sound equipment.

Set construction is carried out at the theatre's Scenic Workshops in a separate building. The sets are then moved to the theatre in time for technical and dress rehearsals.

Personnel

The majority of staff work for the theatre full-time. This includes creative, technical, production, finance and administrative staff who run the theatre and produce the shows, from casting to rehearsing, set building to costume making. However, the acting company changes for each production and actors are therefore only usually contracted for up to seven weeks.

FIND OUT

Useful websites

www.watfordtheatre.co.uk

Questions

Think about a theatre local to you and answer the following questions.

» Is the theatre a producing theatre or a receiving house or both?

» What types, styles and size of shows are programmed at the theatre?

» Is there a pattern to the programming at the theatre? If so, what reasons are there for this?

» How does the theatre market its shows to its audiences?

» Does the theatre do anything to encourage young people into the theatre?

Assessment Tips

To complete this unit you will need to demonstrate understanding of the performance arts and take part in the development, rehearsal and evaluation of a performance. You will have to show that you can identify:

» performance arts forms

» the contexts in which the different performance arts take place

» target audiences.

Through observation, your Journal and your Process Portfolio you will be assessed in:

» taking part in developing and rehearsing a live performance

» contributing ideas during the preparation process and co-operating with others

» responding to direction and instructions

» taking part in a live performance using appropriate techniques

» following procedures, including those related to health and safety.

SUMMARY / SKILLS CHECK

» Performance art?

You should know about:

- ✔ the types of performing arts companies, such as production companies, producing theatres, promoters and music ensembles
- ✔ the various types of show
- ✔ the types of venue (theatres, concert venues), and the different types of stage, and what sorts of shows they are suitable for
- ✔ what audiences want to see.

» Preparations for a live performance

You should know:

- ✔ how to workshop ideas and develop a script
- ✔ about the technical and performance roles and their responsibilities
- ✔ how to schedule the production process
- ✔ how to work effectively during rehearsals
- ✔ how to work safely as a performer and a member of the technical team.

» Taking part in a live performance

You should know:

- ✔ how to be ready for performance – equipment, resources, props and costumes
- ✔ how to keep you and your audience safe
- ✔ the importance of warm ups prior to performance
- ✔ what performance skills will enable you to achieve the higher grades.

» Monitoring and evaluating your work

You should know the importance of:

- ✔ reflection and evaluation
- ✔ getting feedback from your audience
- ✔ reacting to and changing the production process following feedback, reflection and evaluation.

OVERVIEW

Media production includes all sorts of different disciplines. Here are some examples: television, film, audio and radio production, interactive media, photography, computer-game design, animation and creative writing, and they all require their own particular creative skills. You will find that many of these disciplines can be combined – for instance film production requires photography and creative-writing skills, and perhaps animation skills too.

There is one big concept that underpins all these disciplines – this is called **narrative**, which means the way we tell stories. You might not think that a TV ad or a photograph in a magazine is telling a story, but it is. Even if there are no words, we are making the story ourselves from the images, music or design. Remember the dancing Citroën car TV ad? Nowhere did it say: 'Look, this is like a Transformer' – we did that in our own heads.

The skill of the media professional is to tell the stories in such a way that we, the audience, create the story they *want* us to create. They make the potential murderer character in the soap opera creepy and untrustworthy even before we find out that he's been convicted before; they choose the words in the newspaper headlines, and the pictures to illustrate them, which guide us to feel sympathetic or angry or inspired. Nothing in the media 'just happens', or looks the way it does 'because someone simply thought it looked good like that'. Everything has a purpose to help the narrative.

This unit will tell you a little about the institutions that make media productions, the audiences that consume them and how the media represents people, issues and, most importantly, stories. For the successful completion of this unit you will develop skills in media production and use skills from at least two disciplines to create a media product. You must also show that you understand how to review your work.

04

Media Production

Skills list

At the end of this unit you should:

» know about media production

» be able to plan the creation of a media product that combines two or more media disciplines

» be able to create a media product that combines two or more media disciplines

» know how to monitor your own media production work.

Job watch

Jobs in the media range from very highly paid ones to starter jobs; they include:

» runner for a film or TV company

» production assistant

» film, TV or radio producer

» marketing assistant

» web designer

» DJ

» journalist (for magazine, newspaper, radio or TV)

» webzine editor or writer.

Know about media production

How good are you at combining your skills? If you are to successfully complete this unit you must create a media product combining at least two media disciplines. This reflects the real world. Whether it's using creative writing skills to develop a script for a TV drama or making a film using animation, the media professional must be able to combine several different disciplines.

In fact most skills and knowledge in the media industry are linked. The media industry would not be able to survive without the talents of performance and visual artists, for example, and performance and visual art would not survive in the commercial world without the media industry. Although you are being assessed on your media skills for this unit, you will find that the visual or performance arts skills you will gain during the course will really help you develop your work.

Media production disciplines

Before we consider the different media products out there, and the companies that make them, let's remind ourselves of the different disciplines that make up media production.

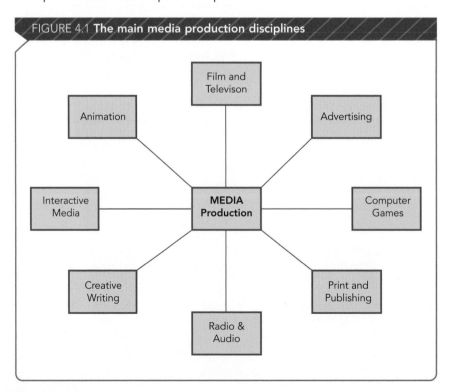

FIGURE 4.1 **The main media production disciplines**

All the cross-over between different disciplines and the skills required by someone working in the creative and media world, only goes to show how important it is for you to be open minded and to develop skills and knowledge in as many areas a possible.

Media products

Before you choose what type of media production you will create, it's important you know about the different types of media products that exist and have some understanding of what they have to offer their audiences. The table below shows a range of different media products. It doesn't include everything as the media industry is constantly changing, being heavily influenced by rapid changes in technology.

TABLE 4.1 **Media products**

TV	Film	Radio	Print-based Media	Media Technology
News	Horror	News	Newspapers	Websites
Documentaries	Comedy	Documentaries	Magazines	CD-ROMs
Sitcoms	Sci-Fi	Soap operas	Comics	Computer games
Soap operas	Fantasy	Sitcoms	Posters	Mobile phones
Drama	Detective	Drama	Print advertisements	DVDs
Current affairs	Romance	Current affairs	Leaflets	
Consumer affairs		Consumer affairs	Books	
Shopping		Quizzes		
Talk shows		Magazine		
Quizzes		Music		
Phone votes		Phone-ins, Discussions		
Community TV				
Music video				
Natural history				

You will see that we have not grouped them within the disciplines, as the disciplines cross-over so many of the products.

Let's look more closely at one discipline – advertising – and how it adapts its products to the medium it is using. Advertising is crucial to the commercial survival of every product. An advertising campaign might appear on TV, in magazines, on radio, online, in cinemas and on posters. A very good example would be the long-running *Talk to Frank* campaign, which tries to encourage people to be responsible about drugs. The message is always the same, but the medium makes the way the story is told quite different. The TV ads are there to attract the viewer's attention, either through humour or shock tactics, while the website gives much more information and the opportunity to confidentially share problems. What works on TV wouldn't work in the online campaign. What you need to do during this unit, is work out what makes each product that you investigate unique. What is it best at doing?

FIGURE 4.2 The *Talk to Frank* anti-drugs campaign uses different media in different ways

Media companies

The media world touches everything we see, hear, experience and do. It influences our opinions and decisions more than you might think, especially in terms of what we spend our money on. Media companies are fully aware of how much power they have to manipulate the consumer.

There are many different types of company in the media world, all with different agendas, priorities and ways of seeing things. Two different companies might tell the same media story in completely different ways because of where they are approaching that story from. A good example of this is when news stories break about politicians or celebrities, different newspapers will react and tell the stories in different ways because of who owns and runs the company, and their particular views.

TEAMWORK

When researching current media products it is important to know about the media production companies that have made the products. In a group, research what the following types of media companies are and how this might affect why and how they make media products. Decide between you how to split up the research and how you are going to communicate your findings back to the whole group.

✻ Public service companies.

✻ Commercial companies.

✻ Independent companies.

✻ Multinational companies.

Record your own findings and the results of your group discussions in your Process Portfolio.

Think about how you will communicate your findings to the rest of the group. Try to be clear and concise, prepare what you are going to say first.

LINKS

Audience

The most important thing to think about in any media product is the audience it is intended for. Without an audience there is no point in the product and if you don't understand the audience you are trying to target then the product will not be successful.

An audience is not just a group of people sat in a theatre or cinema; an audience can be anyone, be they at home watching TV, listening to the radio in the car, looking at a website at work, reading a newspaper on a train or a theatre full of people watching a play – anyone who consumes a media product.

Who is in control?
It would be easy to assume that the audience controls the media, after all we can simply switch off the radio, TV and computer or

leave the cinema if we don't like what we hear and see. But there is much discussion about how the media, in fact, controls its audiences. There is little doubt that the media industry's main purpose is to make you consume more media product. Whether it's the trailers before the main movie in a cinema, the eye-catching headlines on the front page of a newspaper, or the *Big Brother* ten-second theme tune played in-between adverts, weeks even months leading up to a new series, these are all designed to create a sense of 'must have' in the product's audience – to convince you that you need more. Even the cliff-hanger at the end of the soap opera is devised to make you want to see the next episode.

So who *is* in control? Does the media industry mould society, or does it simply reflect it? Take the argument about TV influencing behaviour. Many will say that there is more violence on TV now and that this has lead to increased violence in society, but the media industry argues it is simply reflecting what society is like.

REFLECT

The aim of the computer game 'Grand Theft Auto' is to steal cars and avoid getting caught. Players walk around a city, break into cars and speed away from the police to get back to a hideout for the car to be resprayed – all for money and the kicks of out-running the police.

In a group discuss whether you think this kind of game fulfils players' fantasies so they are less likely to be violent or steal cars, or whether it is more likely to lead players to want the buzz of actually going out and committing the crimes. What do you think of the '18' age-restriction on the game? Is it right to be only for 18-year-olds?

Try to also discuss this with older learners who can legally play the game. Do they respond differently from you?

Listening to others is an important skill. Allow others to speak and don't jump in until they have finished.

LINKS

Who is your audience?

Choice for audiences in media products has been on the increase since the 1960s. With greater choice, comes greater competition, so it has become increasingly important for media producers to understand why people choose one product over another. In other words they need to know about their audience.

Audience figures and analysis are crucial for any media company and research into audiences is taken very seriously within the industry. Some standard questions that need to be asked about an audience are:

» age

» gender – male or female

» sexual preference – heterosexual or homosexual

» ethnicity – race

» nationality – which country they come from

» Standard Occupational Classification (SOC) – what their job is

» disposable income – how much money they have spare after paying bills and living costs.

Of course this doesn't mean that, for instance, all white, heterosexual women over the age of 50 who work in hospitals and have a disposable income of £15,000 a year are guaranteed to want a certain media product – everyone still has their own individual likes and dislikes. Consider your group studying this course; you will all have different preferences for types of music or particular comedy shows, however on the whole there will probably be broad styles that most of you do like. The media are concerned with these broad preferences in audiences, so they can target large parts of the community with a product that will be consumed by the many. Alternatively, they may focus on a niche market that will guarantee profits as no one else is adequately meeting that particular group's needs.

Cable, satellite and now digital TV as well as the Internet, have made this all very complicated as there are now hundreds of stations and innumerable sites that cater to lots of different audiences – some of which are very small niche audiences indeed.

The Internet is also a prime example of showing how different websites are designed for different audiences. Some websites, for instance, will have more of an emphasis on interactivity and gaming, some will be visually arresting while others will be text based with hardly any images, but because they all know their audiences they are all popular.

Researching your audience
You will need to research your potential audience to find out when and where they consume the product and what form and structure

Finding out who your target audience are and what they want from the product is vital. You need to ask, why do people consume media products, and in particular the product you are developing?

they want it in. Then you can identify your target audience, that is who you think you are making your product for. You will also need to consider how this group of people affects the choices you have in creating the product, or how you can affect the audience. For example, are you creating a media product to serve an existing audience or seeking a new audience for your product?

THINK

Consider different TV programmes aimed at your age group. What do audiences get out of watching them that might help you understand why they have been created and why they are successful? Now apply your findings to the media product you are planning. Think about the following questions.

* Who is your target audience?

* Why should they consume your product?

* Have you aimed your product squarely at your target audience? (Think about their age, gender, social class, disposable income, and so on.)

Planning a media production

As part of this unit you will create a media product that combines two of the media disciplines. You will almost certainly produce this work in a team, reflecting the way media production works in the real world.

This probably sounds a daunting task at first, so where do you start? The process can be broken down into various stages:

» generate ideas

» identify your target audience

» research your product

» produce a proposal

» create a team

» identify skills and resources required

» produce a treatment

» draw up a production schedule.

Journal

Part of the assessment process concentrates on your ability to reflect on your work and how you changed what you are doing and why. All through the production process you should monitor and reflect on progress in your Journal as this will form the main evidence for your assessment.

You must therefore think about:

» how well you plan your work

» what you need to change and why

» how well you succeed in achieving your intentions

» what others say about your work.

You need to ensure that your Journal includes evidence of:

» reflections on your work

» decisions taken and reasons for taking them

» changes to the production schedule and reasons for making the changes.

MANAGE

Why not be creative with the way you record and manage information for your Journal and use your mobile phone? You can record your thoughts and ideas and manage information on your progress by taking photos (.jpg), videos (mp4) and recording audio (mp3). You can then transfer these to computer. All these formats are acceptable by Edexcel for submitting evidence as part of Unit 6.

Make sure you manage these resources properly; ensure they are dated and can be clearly identified on your computer for when you need to use them in presentations or your Process Portfolio.

DID YOU KNOW?

Many centres have strict rules about the use of mobile phones; you must seek permission from teachers before getting your phone out in the classroom!

Generating media production ideas

It is more than likely you will be given a brief by your teacher and may even be told which disciplines to work with. For example, you may be asked to create a magazine or produce a radio programme. The possibilities for being creative within the brief you are given are huge – so don't become despondent if you wanted to make a movie but you have been asked to create a website, because with creative thinking you could combine the two.

You will probably make your media product in a team. The best way to start is to get your team together and organise an idea storm. Go back and read the section about 'blue sky thinking' in the previous unit about how to conduct an ideas storm. This will ensure that all your views are heard and respected and will give you the stimulation to come up with some good ideas. However, it is important you are realistic! Any ideas that your group are thinking about making need to be **feasible** with the resources, skills and time you have available.

SWOT analysis

Companies of all shapes and sizes, working in any business will carry out SWOT analysis on their new ideas. SWOT stands for Strengths, Weaknesses, Opportunities and Threats and is a great way of quickly working out whether or not an idea is likely to work.

Here is a SWOT analysis table, with some guidance on what you would put under each heading.

TABLE 4.2 **SWOT** analysis

STRENGTHS	WEAKNESSES	OPPORTUNITIES	THREATS
INTERNAL FACTORS you may have some control or influence		EXTERNAL FACTORS issues that you cannot control	
People in your team have relevant skills, experience and knowledge. You have access to suitable facilities and equipment to make the product. You have good contacts with local companies that make similar products for research.	No one in your team has ever used the product or come into contact with it. Little in-house knowledge of the product or the skills and experience required to make it. Outdated equipment and facilities available to make it.	Evidence that a large audience in your local area would want to consume your product. No competition in your local area for the product – you are targeting a niche market or an audience that is yet to be targeted by others.	High competition from external professional companies. Low demand for the product, small target audience. Local competition can provide product to their audience more cheaply.

THINK

Why not carry out a SWOT analysis of several of the ideas you are considering, to help you decide on the best one to take forward. You may need to carry out some more research to complete your SWOT analysis effectively.

LINKS

Put the results of your SWOT analysis into a word-processed table and keep in your Process Portfolio.

Identifying your target audience

Once you have decided on your product, you will need to consider who is the target audience. It may seem sensible to choose to target an audience that you know most about – your age group! However, you mustn't just assume that you know everything about your age group and their likes and dislikes! You still must ensure that you carry out detailed audience research and keep a record of your findings within your Process Portfolio.

For this reason it may be more interesting to research a different age group or part of the society. For example, could your radio programme or magazine target the new year-sevens or could it be aimed at local businesses to tell them about your school and build relationships?

REMEMBER

Remind yourself about targeting audiences and audience research by looking back at pages 107–110.

Researching your product

Now that you have your product and target audience, you need to research current products on the market to see what approach they have taken, for instance the media language they use to communicate meaning to their audiences. Ask yourself how well will your product fit into this market? Will it provide the same audience appeal? Can you learn anything from any of the similar products out there? Will your product be able to offer anything new?

FIGURE 4.3 **What messages are these magazines putting across?**

Producing a proposal

You've done your ideas storm, researched your initial ideas, decided on a product to fit the brief and targeted your audience. At this stage professional media companies will be expected to produce a **proposal**, which is presented to the writers of the brief – that is the client – or in your case, your teacher. The proposal should show evidence of why you have decided on the final product and your research to back up your decision-making. It should include your SWOT analysis and demonstrate the feasibility of your idea.

Typical contents of a proposal are:

» working title

» medium to be used (TV, radio, print-based media, etc.)

» target audience

» indication of style

» summary of contents

» length/size of product.

Once a proposal has been accepted by your teacher/client it can then be developed into a treatment, which will include:

» costs

» timescales

» creative and production team

» talent (i.e. actors, dancers, etc. if required).

We will look in more detail at treatments later.

ASK

Pick any magazine. Who do you think its intended audience is? How can you tell? Look at:

✳ the name of the magazine

✳ who or what is on the cover

✳ the main colours it uses

✳ the overall design (look at graphics, photos, fonts, etc.)

✳ the language it uses – how complicated is it? How educated would you have to be to understand it fully?

✳ its content.

Show the magazine to some people of different age groups (for instance your parents, grandparents, older or younger brothers or sisters or kids at school). Ask them to look at the same points. Are their impressions the same as yours? What conclusions can you draw from their answers?

Write a short word-processed report on your findings.

LINKS

Creating a team

Before you can start planning production and devising your production schedules you will need to decide on who is doing what. Although you may all have some say in the decisions your group makes, it is sensible to divide responsibilities between your team. You might want to do a quick skills audit to see who would be suitable for which role, and identify any skills gaps. Some of you will almost certainly end up doing more than one job.

You need to know what jobs are required to make your product. Unfortunately this book doesn't have space to list the structure of every different type of media organisation to help you, so you will need to carry out some research yourself to see what jobs there are and how they work together. Your teacher will help you with this during classes, but in the meantime there are lots of places you can look to find out more.

At the end of a movie or TV show, for instance, look at the credits – you may need to record the programme as the credits often are shown very quickly. Is there a difference in job roles and numbers for different types of programme, such as news, documentary or TV drama? All magazines and publications will list the creative team that produced the magazine, sometimes with the pictures of the editors and journalists inside the front cover or at the back of the magazine. There maybe also feature writers, resident journalists or people who write regular columns, scattered through the magazine. A website design company will usually have a list of contacts for the different departments and sometimes the names of people with job titles. Many websites will also credit the designer and have a contact for the webmaster.

But don't forget to consider all the different types of job role that make media production happen, from the finance director to the catering staff, the administrator to the lawyers. If you are at a cinema watching a film, why not watch the full list of credits – you will be amazed at the hundreds of different people that had a part to play in creating the final film. It's not just big blockbusters from Hollywood that have all these different jobs, some roles are needed for any media company. Whatever size your company, someone still has to balance the books and pay the tax man, and someone still has to answer the phones in your office.

Identifying resources

You must now consider what resources you need to complete the product, and when you need them. If you are making a short film, for instance, you will need cameras, but probably not for the entire duration of the project.

Resource management, both of people and equipment, is very important, as both of these are very expensive. You would waste thousands of pounds in the real world if you booked a camera crew and equipment to film but the actors or location were not ready when the crew arrived.

You must research all the equipment and resources you think you will need, make sure you can get hold of them when and where you need them, and work out how much they will cost. Hopefully your centre will be able to provide most of the things you require, but don't forget that in the real world these will cost money. You must make sure the equipment is available when you need it. If several of you are hoping to use computers or cameras, for instance, you have to make sure you don't clash with timings when you want to use them. Work out your schedule for the use of resources carefully, and check with others who might be using the same equipment. If you have a detailed production schedule, you should be able to see when you need certain resources, so write it down and then book them!

Certain people are only needed at certain times. A film editor, for instance, might be involved during the early planning stages of a production but not required again until the film is in the can. It would be an absolute waste of money for the editor to be paid and employed for the whole duration of the production when they have nothing to do until the end.

Don't forget to think about the detail, the small items you might forget but that are absolutely crucial. Professionals are thorough in their preparation, and ensure they don't forget anything. How embarrassing would it be if you got to the set to film and you had no tapes or film for your cameras?

Producing a treatment

Your **treatment** is an expanded version of your proposal, which has now, hopefully, been accepted by your teacher/client. A treatment should demonstrate that you have thought of everything

JOURNAL TIPS

Whenever you talk to someone about researching the available resources, make sure you keep detailed notes of what was discussed in your Journal to refer back to and use in meetings.

and will be an excellent way of producing evidence for your Process Portfolio and ensuring the production runs smoothly.

Your treatment should include:

» research – primary and/or secondary

» draft scripts

» visuals – **mood-** and **story-boards**

» creative and production team list – contact details, job roles, etc.

» talent – contact details, roles

» costs and budget including **contingency plans**

» sources – who are you using for information and/or resources.

You can also include documents that are more specific to the disciplines and product you are working within, these are discussed in the next part of this chapter.

Drawing up a production schedule

Can a newspaper risk being late in going to the printers? Do you think that a national paper is ever late going to the newsstands – it's unthinkable! Well you need to take the production or your product just as seriously.

As with the creation of any creative and media product, especially when working as part of a team, a detailed **production schedule** is vital. Knowing when everything needs to get done by and by whom, will ensure you hit your deadlines and keep the client happy.

FIGURE 4.4 A production timeline helps you to clearly see the progress of your production

Production Schedule – Local Football Club Documentary / Item	Mon, 12 June	Tues, 13 June	Wed, 14 June	Thurs, 15 June	Fri, 16 June	Mon, 12 June	Tues, 13 June	Wed, 14 June	Thurs, 15 June	Fri, 16 June	Mon, 12 June	Tues, 13 June	Wed, 14 June	Thurs, 15 June	Fri, 16 June
1. Research															
1.1 Club History	■	■													
1.2 Football History	■	■	■													
1.3 Sourcing Archive Film						■	■	■	■	■	■	■	■	■	
2. Filming															
2.1 Filming Matches	■			■											
2.2 Filming Interviews						■	■	■							
3. Photography															
3.1 Scanning old photos											■				

A timeline is a useful way to see where, when and how each person's role depends on another's, and how if one person does not stick to the schedule it will have a knock-on effect elsewhere. You can also see when each person has more responsibility and more to do, so you can direct others who are less busy to support them.

Production documents

Other paperwork or planning documents you may have to produce will depend on the disciplines you are working within. Industry people do not have the time to produce documents and paperwork simply for the sake of it, so the documents they do produce save valuable time and money in the production process. If you ignore the need to produce any of the following that your teacher asks you to, you run the risk of wasting time and energy and, in the real world, money, further down the line. Therefore it's important you start now to get into good practice for your career in the creative and media industry.

Some examples of specialist documents are:

» treatment

» budget

» **shooting script**

» **cue sheets**

» **location recce**

» **schematic** – for a website

» page layout

» **risk assessments**.

All of these require extra work and research, however the more you plan the easier it will be to create your product.

Creating your media product

You should now be well on the way to starting production and, as always, the more prepared you are the more enjoyable this part of the process will be. However, never think that you stop researching and developing your ideas for your product.

JOIN IN

To be successful in group-work and in completing a successful product, it is important that you take an active part in the process. Many people are shy or unconfident and therefore will tend to hover on the sidelines of activities and meetings, letting those who think they know it all take over. However difficult you may find it try to make an effort to push yourself forward and suggest ideas, discuss issues, negotiate and present a different point of view from others around you. It is not only vital for your personal assessment and development but crucial for the success of the project.

If you are someone who has no trouble at all putting your point of view, try to encourage others less confident than yourself. It is everyone's responsibility to ensure opportunities are made for each and every member of the team to be heard and supported.

Following the production schedule

Having a production schedule and following it are two completely different matters. Every time something changes, or part of the production doesn't go to plan, you will need to adjust your production schedule. This may mean that later processes, such as editing, get squeezed – this is a pity as a good period of time in post-production (what goes on after the film/programme/website/song, etc. is made) is vital to ensure a professional-looking product – however, it happens and the editors or designers need to be warned if this is likely so that they can be prepared.

Throughout the production process you need to ensure that you regularly:

» monitor the production schedule to see if you are on time and hitting deadlines

JOURNAL TIPS

It's not always easy to remember why production schedules are changed, so make sure you keep notes of the reasons for your changes in your Journal.

- keep a record of everything in your Journal
- log materials – you will collect lots of recordings, photos, etc. – make sure you know what is what, or you will be in a mess when you start editing your work for the final product
- review materials – make sure you look at what you have filmed or the photos you have collected and make decisions as you go along on what might be used and what probably won't and if you need to shoot or record anything again
- present rough drafts to your team or your teacher regularly to get feedback.

Always make sure you keep a record of any changes for your Process Portfolio; date them and say what version they are next to the title of the project.

FIGURE 4.5 **Clearly identifying the date and version number of your documents will help with your planning and post-production**

Production Schedule (V2.6)

Production: **Local Arts Forum Website** Last updated: **4/17/08**

As you can see in Figure 4.5 we have used both ways to show the different versions of the production schedule. This version is V2.6, this means that there have been two major revisions of the production schedule and six minor changes. If you are simply dating your production schedule (and often this is a lot simpler), you must make sure that it is clear that the date is when the production schedule was last updated and not simply when the schedule starts or the date it was created.

The production schedule can become very complicated, especially as many of the jobs that need to be done will overlap. Figure 4.6 should help make clearer the stepping-stones for completing your production, whatever it may be, and you must base your production schedule on this and plan accordingly.

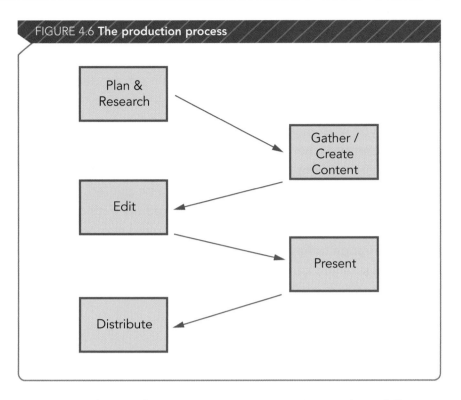

FIGURE 4.6 **The production process**

Keeping to the production process in Figure 4.6, and carefully monitoring your production schedule throughout, should lead to a less stressful completion of your product.

Completing your product

It's very easy to get excited about running around and filming, or taking photos for your leaflets or magazines, or recording in a music studio with a band. But once you have captured and created your content you must allow enough time to edit and put together your final product. Post-production is the term commonly used for the processes that go into this finishing of a media product – particularly film, TV and sound products. It occurs after you have finished gathering and/or creating the content elements and includes the editing and adding of the finishing touches, such as page numbers, captions, colour or sound balance and so on. Remember, the post-production phase is important in all media projects from finishing a website to completing your leaflet design.

You must ensure that you allow enough time for post-production processes, such as editing. Finishing the final design for your leaflet or magazine the night before the deadline, for instance, is not going to give you enough time to make sure that the content is accurate and you have spell checked it correctly.

REMEMBER

Spell checkers are useful to help you check your word-processed work, but remember they won't check you have got the right word. If you have typed 'form' instead of 'from', for instance, a spell check won't pick it up, so always read through your work carefully as well or get someone else to check it too.

Production and distribution

Once you have created a magazine or a film or built a website on your computer, you need to also ensure that it can produced and distributed in an appropriate manner.

To do this you must make sure you fully understand from the brief how your client/teacher wishes the final product to be presented. If it's a magazine it might be as simple as creating a PDF that can go to your centre's reprographics department to be printed, and copies placed in the entrance hall to be picked up. If it's a film you need to ensure you can copy it on to the required number of DVDs, or arrange to have it shown to the intended audience. You must make sure you know how your final product should be delivered and how it will be distributed.

Safe working practices

Working safely is really important for everyone and you should reflect on what you did to ensure the safety of the production in your Journal. You might want to refer back to the safety section in Unit 3.

Here are some guidelines to consider as a media specialist.

» Be careful lifting heavy equipment, always make sure you have enough people to help you.

» Media professionals have to walk around for long periods with bags full of equipment, on their shoulders. Be careful even with small bags to carry them properly and with good posture. If you don't use the correct straps and bags this can be just as damaging to your body as lifting heavy equipment incorrectly.

» Make sure electrical equipment you are using is PAT tested. There should be a sticker on the plug of every piece of equipment to tell you whether it's been tested within the last 12 months.

» Ensure there are no trailing cables and wires that could become trip hazards for your cast and crew.

» It can be very tempting when trying to get a good camera angle to try all sorts of interesting shots from a height. Don't use ladders without proper supervision. There are very strict rules about working at heights. If in doubt, wait to talk to a member of

Did You Know?

As part of your work for Unit 5 you may be expected to present your work in a suitable manner. Therefore it's crucial you understand how to get your product off computers in a format that can be used and shown to other people.

staff. Do not stand on chairs or tables to carry out technical work.

» Media specialists often have to work long hours at a computer, whether its script writing, animating, or editing film or music. Make sure you take regular breaks, that you have a good posture when sitting at the computer, and have your eyes tested regularly.

» Behave professionally at all times and understand that you need to be able to trust each other. Some work can be dangerous and equipment can easily get damaged if you are not all concentrating and looking after each other's safety as well as your own.

» Every production should have a risk assessment done before work commences. Your educational centre will have examples of how to do this.

» Media professionals have to be very careful about filming or recording members of the public, especially if they are under 18. You cannot simply go out and film anyone in the street without getting their permission. If they are under 18 then their parents need to give permission. Media companies will have what is called a 'Model Release Form' for the member of the public to sign when they have been interviewed or filmed.

For further information on current legislation and handouts, visit the Health and Safety Executive website at www.hse.gov.uk

JOURNAL TIPS

Always keep a log of any health and safety concerns that arise during the production process, and what you do to solve them.

FIGURE 4.7 **Always take great care when working at height**

Remember that as a media student you are very visible to the general public, mainly because when you are working you will probably have a film camera, microphones and other equipment with you. Therefore you have to be even more careful than any other young person to be polite and professional when working in very public areas. You are on show, and you are not only representing yourself but your group and your centre. Therefore always get permission to work on location, discuss what you want to do in advance with your teacher and behave appropriately at all times.

Monitoring and evaluating your work

If you have been keeping a detailed Journal as suggested at the beginning of this unit then you will be half way to completing what you need to prove for this part of your assessment. You should be able to reflect on the following questions:

» How well did your plan go?

» What did you need to change and why?

» What went well and what did not?

» How well do you feel you did?

» What did others say about your work?

Don't forget you could do a skills audit or carry out a 360-degree feedback on your work within this unit and on the final media production.

It's really important that you understand how to review your progress and react to your findings so as to improve. No one gets everything right first time in the creative arts; you will experience a lot of trial and error. What is far more important is the ability to review your work and make decisions to improve it or do things differently in the future. Be as objective about your own work as you would be of others' work, rather than subjective and too conscious of your own feelings and insecurities.

Ask yourself, how good were you at:

» completing each task to the best of your abilities

» meeting deadlines

» suggesting ideas

» practising and developing your skills

» completing what you were supposed to complete

» keeping a detailed Journal

» listening to ideas, advice and guidance?

What the professionals do

When a new movie or TV programme has been made the production company will often hold special screenings for an invited group of a cross-section of the target audience. After the screening they will ask the audience to complete a questionnaire about it. The responses to these questionnaires could have a big impact on the final media production and even at this late stage the company may decide to re-edit the film, delaying the release.

This kind of research and evaluation takes place across all media products, where companies will have regular focus groups to evaluate the success of their product before distribution.

REFLECT

Organise a preview and questionnaire for your product. Fully document this and say how you would change things in the light of the responses to improve the production or your own performance.

Example questions for you to think about in your evaluation:

* Is the finished product fit for purpose?

* Did it communicate with the target audience?

* Did the content meet the needs of the brief?

* Did you group work effectively as a team to create the finished product?

* What would your group do differently next time?

You could try doing one or two face-to-face interviews based on your questionnaire. This will help develop your speaking and listening skills.

LINKS

Ask your supervisor at your work experience placement to help you find out:

» Who is the company's target audience?

» What does the company do to target them?

» Does the company ever carry out a SWOT analysis on the company or its products/services? If not, does it use any other ways to assess whether they are successful or meeting the needs of the audience?

» What media skills are required by staff at the company?

I want to be...

... a radio presenter

» **How did you get into radio?**

I did a BTEC Media course and a Performing Arts course, then worked for free at a radio station gaining valuable skills and knowledge. I did everything and anything (including bin emptying and floor cleaning). I eventually proved myself and started presenting late night or very early morning shows.

» **What are your responsibilities at Fox FM?**

I am currently a Station Producer and Drivetime Host. I create production for my show and for the station as a whole, even adverts sometimes. Production can vary from a song parody to a comical sketch, it depends what is topical at the time.

» **Do you work in a team?**

I have a travel girl on my show and we have to work as a team passing travel information to each other and planning any links I am to involve her in. Apart from that, most of my work is done just by me.

» **Do you have to regularly show your work to others at the radio station during the creative process?**

I have a 'snoop' every week, this is an air-check with my line manager, making sure I am keeping things tight and on track.

» **What's the hardest thing about your job?**

Sounding happy on air when you are not. Everyone has bad days, even presenters, but you can't bury your head in a paper or in your computer like you can in other jobs.

» **What creative or technical skills do you need to be a good radio presenter?**

On air you need to be confident, real, honest, knowledgeable in music and likable. Production-wise you need to know how the latest editing programs work and be VERY computer literate!

» **When developing creative work, where do you draw inspiration or ideas from?**

Listening to your competitors is VERY important, if someone is doing something well, think how you can recycle what they do and even make it better. Ideas are everywhere.

» **What is the biggest influence on your creative and development decisions?**

My colleagues. I LOVE being told to do something better as long as I am told HOW to make it better.

www.foxfm.co.uk
www.myspace.com/debbieandadam

✱ Adam Ball

Case Study

Clock – Digital Marketeers →

Founded in 1997 originally as a Prince's Trust start-up business Clock is an award-winning web-marketing company, based in Hertfordshire. The company also has an office in Shanghai, China.

Creating Online Marketing

The company designs, builds, hosts, maintains and markets its clients' products. When starting the production process of a new website the company clearly establishes the goal and purpose of the site first before starting the design work.

Clients

Clients include banks, Abbey and Barclays; Teenage Cancer Trust; comedians' websites, such as Eddie Izzard and Little Britain; Rugby Reunited; newspapers *The Times* and the *Sun*; TV company websites, such as the BBC, Tiger Aspect and Endemol; and games companies Sega and PlayStation.

Facilities

Since 2002 the company has occupied an old school house in Hertfordshire, which includes open-plan offices and a boardroom.

Personnel

The company started with just one computer in Managing Director and founder, Syd Nadim's, flat. The company now employs over 30 full-time staff, and has a turnover of around £2 million. Clock employees have a balance of creative and technical abilities, covering digital, marketing and advertising expertise in the following departments:

» Sales – business development and account management

» Project management – including management of the studio

» Studio – creative and development team

» Finance

» Administration – including personnel management

» Information systems.

Clock actively encourages its creative and development team to keep up to date with developments in digital media so that they can pass these on to their clients. To see examples of their work, visit www.clock.co.uk.

Questions

Visit some of the websites designed by Clock and consider the following questions:

» What specific media skills do you need to create a successful website?

» What makes a successful website? And what makes it not?

» What research skills would be required for people working in the different departments of Clock?

» What ways could you advertise and market your own online product?

To complete this unit you will need to demonstrate your understanding of media production and take part in the development and production of a media product that combines at least two disciplines.

You must present a Process Portfolio that includes the following:

» Research into media products – this can be presented as a written document, oral presentation, web page or blog.

» Research for your finished media production (presented in either verbal or written form).

» All your ideas and evidence of explorations of the ideas for your final media product.

» Your planning documentation – scripts, story-boards, resource requirements, resource bookings, shooting schedules, production schedule, etc.

» Your post-production documentation – shooting logs, edit decisions, lists, editing notes.

» Your Journal recording all your reflections on what you have done.

» The finished media product.

The content of your Process Portfolio can be presented in many different ways, so consider using the new technologies that are now so readily available, such as web pages, blogs or e-portfolios.

Don't forget, your professionalism during the production process is key to the successful completion of the unit. Not only will good attendance, punctuality and attitude allow you the time and focus to work effectively, but your ability to turn up on time could affect part of your assessment by your teacher.

SUMMARY / SKILLS CHECK

» Know about media production

You should know about the:

✓ different media products within TV, film, radio, print-based media and interactive media technology

✓ audience that your media production is intended for, including how to research your target audience and find out why they are interested in certain products.

» Planning a media production

You should know:

✓ how to generate media production ideas, research them and decide which are feasible

✓ how to create a proposal for your media product

✓ how to research the jobs involved for your media production

✓ how to create your team

✓ how to develop your treatment and production schedule

✓ what other professional documentation is required for your media product

✓ how to manage resources.

» Creating your media product

You should know:

✓ how to keep on-track and follow your production schedule

✓ how to make your final product ready for distribution

✓ how to distribute it appropriately

✓ about safe working practices.

» Monitoring and evaluating your work

You should know:

✓ the importance of reflection and evaluation

✓ the importance of reacting and changing the production process in the light of reflection and evaluation.

OVERVIEW

If you are going to work in creative and media you are, at some point, going to have to present your work to an audience if you are to earn a living. Whether you are a performer, fine artist, graphic designer, TV or radio producer or even a web designer, you will need the appropriate presentation skills. This unit is going to help you consider:

» how your production should be presented

» how to publicise it to your target audience.

This unit runs in parallel with Units 2, 3 or 4 and also leads on to the final unit of the Diploma – Unit 6: Skills Report. You will use the work you have produced in one of the previous units (Visual Arts, Performance Arts or Media Production) for both this unit and Unit 6. You will research ways in which this product would be presented in the professional industry and then manage the process to present your own work in an appropriate way.

Some of the preparation for this unit will be done as you are completing your work for Units 2, 3 or 4. In order to do this you must ensure you keep detailed Process Portfolios in all units.

This unit is a fantastic introduction for all those entrepreneurs out there who want to make money out of the creative hard work you will put into making your products. Although it is vital to learn how to be creative, make a product and carefully research your target audience, what's the point if you don't know how to complete the production process – tell the audience about your product and sell it to them?

It is important to remember that this unit does not assess the *quality* of the actual work being presented; this will have already been assessed as part of specialist Units 2, 3 or 4. To achieve this unit you must take as much care with presenting your work as you did making it in the first place.

So stand by for a quick guide to completing this exciting unit, which will help you in the future to make money out of your creativity!

05

Presentation

Skills list

At the end of this unit you should:

» be able to plan the presentation of your own creative and media work in an appropriate form

» know how to publicise the presentation

» be able to present your own creative and media work.

Job watch

Job roles in the creative and media industry that require presentation skills include:

» theatre/venue manager

» finance director

» music promoter

» publisher

» broadcaster

» film, TV or radio producer

» gallery owner

» curator.

Planning your presentation

When you start this unit, you will probably be in one of the following two positions – work out which you are:

1. You have been told by your teacher that you will be assessed on the presentation of the finished work for one of the optional units (Units 2, 3 or 4) as part of this unit – Unit 5. Therefore the time you will spend on the product and presenting it will be longer than your other optional unit.

2. You have completed Unit 1, and both your optional units (Units 2, 3 or 4). Your teacher will then tell you to choose which product you have made during the course to present and be assessed for this unit.

If you have been asked to choose, then you need to seriously consider your options before continuing. Why not carry out a SWOT analysis of your products before you decide (see Unit 4). Remember that you are not looking at the Strengths, Weaknesses, Opportunities and Threats of the actual work to be presented – this is not being assessed in this unit – but options for its presentation. Given the skills, resources and facilities you have to hand, you need to analyse whether it is better to present your performance work, your visual arts product or your media product.

What is a presentation?

A presentation is simply showing something to an audience. The presentation of your creative and media work can take a variety of forms depending on the type of product. The most obvious form is for performance art. If you have completed Unit 3: Performance Arts, then it is likely that you will have devised a show for an audience. Within this unit you would look in detail at how to decide on a venue for the show, when your performance unit will be, how to make people aware of the performance and how to ensure the performance takes place in a professional and appropriate manner.

This is a very obvious scenario, but some of the other media products might not be so straightforward. How, for example, would you present a series of short films or radio programmes if your centre does not have its own TV or radio station to broadcast them on?

JOURNAL TIPS

If your venue has already been decided during the completion of the performance art unit, make sure you give the reasons why that particular decision was made. You could also offer some ideas of other suitable venues. Record all these thoughts and decision processes in your Journal.

Working in a team

Whether your product was created in a group or on your own, to successfully complete this unit it is likely you will carry out your presentation as part of a team. The creative process itself can often be quite a lonely one. Hopefully, you will find working within a team to make your presentation a stimulating and positive influence on your work and the completion of the tasks. The writing team for this book, for example, couldn't have worked successfully or felt happy in what they were achieving without constantly swapping emails with each other. The book then required support from other professionals, such as the publishers, editors, designers, illustrators and picture researchers who put the final product together. Therefore, although it doesn't necessarily need a team effort to make a creative and media product or its individual parts, it usually does require a team effort to present it!

FIGURE 5.1 **Teamworking is an integral part of the creative and media industry**

Remember that working in a group means that you can:

» have wider experience, knowledge and skills to draw upon

» share ideas

» encourage each other

» stimulate debate for decision-making

» get clarification

» get support from others.

Academic courses tend to focus on the work of the individual. This is mainly because it is much easier to assess and examine the individual through essays and exam papers. However, working as a team reflects the typical working life of a creative and media professional, so teamwork is something you must learn how to do. However, you will need to help your teachers and external examiners see what is your own work within the team. It is absolutely crucial, if you want to be awarded the grades you deserve, that you keep individual detailed notes and a Process Portfolio during the management of this presentation.

Meetings

Once you have a clear idea about which product to present, you need to plan all the processes that will lead up to making the presentation. This is especially important if you are working as a team, as everyone needs to know what is happening and who is doing what and when. One of the best ways to keep track of progress is to hold regular meetings.

As part of your Diploma work you need to organise, attend and contribute to planning meetings. It is very important that meetings are productive and not simply a vague chat or discussion that goes on and on. In the professional world 'time is money' and meetings are, in fact, seen as being very expensive, as each person involved is away from their telephone, desk, workstation, email and therefore away from making money for the company.

Meetings must be productive and have clear aims and objectives as to why you have brought everyone together. They should not simply become an opportunity for moans and groans! Meetings should:

» assess progress

» identify problems

» resolve issues

» make decisions.

Good, concise meetings that clarify issues and make decisions are essential if a company is to be successful and competitive. To ensure a successful meeting try to stick to the following guidelines:

» keep it short – one hour maximum

» have clear aims and **objectives**

» have a clear **agenda** – list of the topics to be covered

» have a chairperson – their role is to time-keep, ensure that discussions don't go off the topic, and allow for everyone to be heard – not simply the loudest and most dominant!

» take **minutes** – in the professional world this would usually be done by an administrator who doesn't take part in discussions. They write notes on what has been decided, record who is to take what action and distribute a copy of these notes to all who attended the meeting. However you will all be keeping your own minutes as part of your Journal and Process Portfolio.

A meeting can be of any size in any location, it doesn't have to be the whole group in a formal meeting as described above. A chat about your project between two members of the team in the school canteen or in a corridor can be classed as a meeting. This is typical professional practice – if you have a question why wait until the next formal meeting to ask it? However, make sure you don't forget to write down what was said and what was decided! You may need the evidence later during a formal meeting when something hasn't got done! It's a good idea to drop an email confirming what was said.

JOURNAL TIPS

Don't rely on photocopying other people's notes of meetings for your Process Portfolio – this is not suitable evidence. You have to take your own notes, especially as you are likely to be carrying out individual roles within the team.

FIGURE 5.2 **An agenda and minutes from a progress meeting**

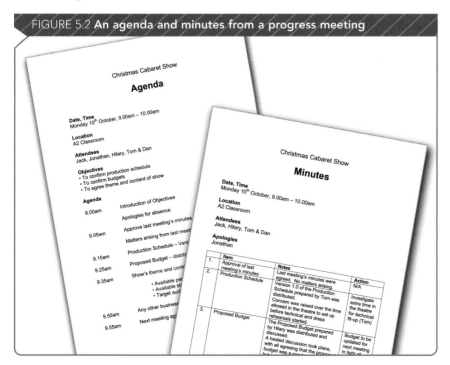

Recording your meetings

Paperwork for meetings can include:

» agenda – to give a clear idea of what is to be discussed this time

» minutes of the last meeting – so you can see what was said and decided last time

» supporting paperwork – for instance schedules, quotes, reports.

Agenda

Setting and sending out an agenda before the meeting will ensure that everyone will come prepared. This will lead to more focused discussions making it easier to come to decisions. For example, if you know that you will be discussing proposed venues and ticket prices then you can all ensure that you attend the meeting having researched possible venues and what prices you can reasonably charge your target audience. This will speed up the decision-making process.

Minutes

The agenda will also help you to structure the minutes of the meeting. Minutes should not be a word-for-word account of all that was discussed; they should only record important information, such as what was discussed, any decisions that were made and who is to action those decisions. It is crucial that everyone knows what needs to be done, by whom and by when.

Task allocation is very important, be clear on:

» what the task is – give enough detail for the person undertaking it to manage it successfully

» who is going to complete the task

» what the deadlines are.

Make sure tasks are allocated fairly among the group and that everyone has an equal share of the responsibilities.

Successful teamworking

Working successfully in a team requires a range of skills. You need to keep focused on the task, communicate clearly and listen effectively to your team-mates. It helps to be open to constructive criticism yourself and sensitive about dishing out your own criticism. Keep your comments constructive and aimed squarely at achieving the successful completion of the task.

DID YOU KNOW?

If meetings are effective you don't need to have so many of them and can actually be more productive.

Listening

Listening to what people are actually saying and making sure you understand them seems obvious, but this is where most problems arise when working as part of a team. It is all too easy for confusion or a misunderstanding to waste much valuable time, and it is nearly always down to some people talking too much, others not talking at all, or people not listening properly and taking time to ensure they understand each other.

To be a good listener:

1 Try not to interrupt others while they are speaking.

2 Look interested, be encouraging.

3 Make eye contact.

4 Don't whisper or fidget while others are talking.

To be a good communicator:

1 Try to talk *to* people, not *at* them.

2 Be clear in your head what you want to say before you start.

3 Speak clearly – and not too fast – keep jargon to a minimum.

4 Make eye contact.

5 Involve your listeners, make them feel part of your idea.

We communicate not only by words but also by body language. Why not video a meeting – use a static wide shot of the room so camera can see everyone.

As a group, watch the video and observe how everyone is positioned in the room. Are they sitting or standing? Do they look relaxed or tense? Look at how people react with their body language. Ask how the person talking felt at the time.

You will find this really useful to see what you do with your body language, perhaps without even realising. Do you think you should try and alter your body language? Think about how your body language makes you feel and the effect it has on others. Was everyone involved? Was everyone encouraged to join in? If not, how can you participate more fully next time, or encourage others to join in just by altering your body language?

Giving and receiving criticism

Whatever your age or experience, receiving criticism can be difficult. You only have to watch an episode of the BBC show *The Apprentice* to witness experienced and successful professionals dishing out criticism but being bad at receiving it objectively!

However, the giving and receiving of constructive criticism is invaluable for the success of the project, and is part of everyday life in creative and media companies. So what can you do to ensure you are acting responsibly and fairly when criticising others? Well, for a start, don't make it personal! For example, don't say, 'You did that wrong', 'You look bored', 'You never like my ideas' or 'I could have done better in my sleep!' Try to make your comments objective, for instance: 'I don't think that is going to work', then give some practical reasons why it won't work. Criticism should always be about fact – was something late, was the work not completed, was it of poor quality and if so why?

How can you improve your ability to receive criticism? Here are some tips. Try to:

» listen

» take time to digest information

» thank the person for caring to comment and help

» ask questions if anything isn't clear.

If the criticism is fair, then accept it and use it to help you do a better job next time.

DON'T simply turn around and say something aggressive back. You will find in life that the person who 'loses it' and gets angry usually does so out of defence because they know they have a weak argument.

If the criticism is quite serious and you find it difficult to respond on the spot, then ask to feed back at the next meeting or talk to the person giving the criticism the next day. This will give you time to absorb the comments and decide for yourself whether or not it was fair.

It can be very difficult for anyone of any age to be objective and actually listen properly to criticism. It can help to ask someone else who was at the meeting to give their interpretation of what was being criticised to help you understand.

What doesn't help...

Don't go into a meeting or practical session being competitive and scoring points against others in the group – it is not a competition between each of you. The point is for the team effort to be successful. Much better to support each other so you can all be as good as possible; there is nothing stopping all of you getting top grades, the qualification is not like running a race!

A meeting or practical session can be ruined by members of the group regularly turning up late, leaving early or going for long breaks. Secretive whispering and discussions between just a few people is really rude and can divide the group, so don't let it happen. If something is worth saying then everyone should hear it.

Personal prejudices against other individuals in the group are particularly destructive. It can result in you closing yourself off from excellent creative ideas, so always show respect to everyone and give them a chance. Everyone in your group is, after all, a potential colleague and so their views are important.

Research the venue or location for your presentation

Once you have decided what to present, you need to think about where to present it. A suitable venue is essential.

You will probably hold the presentation at your centre, however researching local professional venues will help you understand the specific requirements of presenting your creative and media product. This is very important for your success in this unit. You never know, during your research you might even find someone willing to allow you to use their venue.

For example, if you need to display your work in a gallery-type environment in your centre, but have simply been given choices of some classrooms to use, then you will need to work hard to transform the classroom into a space that looks and feels like a gallery. Some rooms will be better for this than others, however if you have never been in a gallery how will you know which to choose and what the room should end up looking like?

For some media work you might not know what type of venue you need as you are still struggling with how it could be presented. A visit to a gallery such as Tate Modern might help, as fine art is not simply a collection of paintings hung on a wall any more. Media art is growing in popularity and you might get some great ideas on how to display your digital media work from visiting contemporary spaces and exhibitions. It is important you don't assume anything about what venues are like, because it is very likely that when you did last visit a theatre, gallery or cinema, for example, that you were more concerned with observing the work than what the rooms, facilities and staffing were like. So get out there and do some field work!

Nearly every community will have a theatre, cinema or gallery – all obvious venues for presenting work. However, you need to think more widely than this as many products from the creative and media disciplines would not typically be found in these venues. Some products, for instance, would typically be presented in a shop for audiences to buy, some would be on community notice boards around the town, some even in your own home on your computer through the Internet – a venue could be online!

So why not have a brain-storm session to think of all the different places your product would usually be shown to people (presented to an audience).

ASK

Visit a professional venue. Remember, you are trying to discover what makes the venue suitable for presenting media products and why it is appropriate to your audience. These are the ingredients you need to recreate in your venue back at your centre. Look at:

✱ size of venue – how many seats, space for each exhibitor

✱ resources – chairs, staging, screens

✱ equipment – projectors, computers, lighting, sound

✱ staffing – projectionists, sound and lighting engineers, ushers

Even how many plugs are available is important.

Try to talk to the manager of the venue to ask specific questions. See if they might show you round. And don't forget to collect examples of any publicity materials that the professional venue produces – this will come in handy for your Process Portfolio.

Record your findings as notes, recordings and/or photographs.

LINKS

Negotiation

Armed with the information from your site visit you now need to secure your venue. This might be a very simple process as your choices may be limited. Most schools and colleges only have one performance space and therefore availability will be limited, so you may simply be negotiating when you can have access to rehearse and perform. However, other negotiations might take longer if you ask for something unusual. For example, you may decide you would like your animations or short films to be projected onto the outside of a college building, or to perform street theatre in the grounds of your school, or negotiate with another teacher a more suitable room to create your gallery. Your group might want to present an 'Oscars'-style evening using the centre's theatre.

Before you go into negotiations to ask for anything, you must be clear about:

» when you need the venue (DON'T FORGET setting up and taking down time)

» what facilities you require

» what equipment you require

» what staffing, if any, you require.

Of course, it may not be physical space you are negotiating for. You may need to negotiate with your centre's IT department, for instance, for web space to host your online presentation.

Preparing your product

You now know what product you are presenting and where and when it will be presented. However, before publicising it you must consider whether you will need to do anything to the product to ensure it is suitable for presentation in the way you intend. Here are some things you might want to think about.

» Computer files come in all sorts of different formats – what format, for instance, do you need the work to be in so that it can be presented online?

» Does the design work on you computer need to be printed out? If so, do you have a printer available to do this? Will you need an external company to do this for you? This could cost a lot both in money and time!

» Will your performance fit into the venue you have booked?

» Does your artwork need to be framed or mounted?

» Does your 3D work need a plinth or platform to stand on?

» Will you need any help during the presentation? For instance, someone to take tickets or show people around?

If you are having problems, don't forget to record your experiences in your Journal. It's a fact of life that things don't always go to plan; the real test is how you deal with such difficulties, and how creative and determined you are in overcoming them. The evidence you record in your Journal will help with both your evaluation and with the final assessment of your work for this unit.

Publicising your presentation

Publicising the presentation of your production is the link between knowing your audience, which you will have researched as part of creating your product, and meeting that audience's needs.

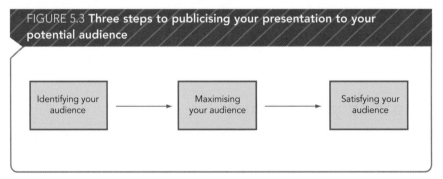

FIGURE 5.3 **Three steps to publicising your presentation to your potential audience**

Publicity is about ensuring as many people as possible know about your product. To do this you have to focus on why your product will be of interest to the audience you are targeting.

Professional companies always look for the 'USP' – **Unique Selling Point** – of their product. This is the thing that makes their product special. Then they need to think about how to tell their target audience about the USP or their product. If you are advertising your product to the correct people and telling them what they want to hear then you will hopefully have created the best opportunity to maximise your audience.

Sometimes the USP for a product is different depending on whom you are targeting. If you have a new product for children, the USP to the kids may be that it looks great and everyone in the playground will think you look cool, while the USP you promote in publicity aimed at the parents may focus on how much safer your product is than other products.

So how do you maximise your audience? Through good targeted, appropriate and creative publicity! After all, what's the point of doing all this work if no one will see your presentation? Why not think big? Think crowds, think sell-out – but don't over-sell your presentation by lying!

How to publicise creative and media events

The best way to understand how to target your audience is to research what usually works in the real world. When you visit theatres, galleries, cinemas, shops why not make a habit of collecting their publicity materials.

Companies don't just publicise their products in one way, they will often have a marketing plan that surrounds their audiences with their product so there is no way you cannot know a new book, film, album, etc. is on sale.

Consider a new film that is due to be released. Months before it opens in cinemas you will start to hear about it through adverts in newspapers and on TV; trailers of the film will be played in cinemas sometimes six months or even more before the release date. DVDs of films by the same distributors will also advertise up-and-coming films. You can see trailers on the production company's website and sometimes download them on iTunes before the film is released. When the film finally opens, you will find actors on every TV show being interviewed with clips from the film; McDonald's will be giving away branded toys from China with their Happy Meals; posters will appear on bus stops, tube trains and buildings. Everything possible to surround you with information about this product is done, creating anticipation and building up a desire for that product. Then, after only a few months, the whole process is repeated as the DVD is released ready for Christmas.

You may have heard the term 'teaser campaign' used to describe publicity that comes out before a product is available. Often this publicity is very sketchy and is really to hook people into being interested in a product. The Internet has become an excellent tool for this, especially with social networking websites such as YouTube. A video clip that hints at a long-awaited new album or film will mysteriously find its way onto a website – I wonder who put it there or started the rumour?

FIGURE 5.4 **Professional publicity uses several different ways to promote a media product, such as branded merchandise**

T H I N K

When did you last consume a creative and media product? Think about:

✳ Did you have a choice of product?

✳ If so, why did you choose one product over another?

Planning your promotional activities

So what is the best way to publicise *your* presentation? Whatever it is, it won't be in just one way. Like the industry, you need to have a plan that includes several promotional activities, linked together so your audience understands that they are promoting the same product.

TEAMWORK

In your team start researching products similar to yours.

How are they publicised to their audiences?

In how many different ways are they promoted?

You could divide up this task, sending individuals off to work alone. However, consider the benefits of two or three of you going into a town centre together to research a product. You might find it easier to stay focused on the tasks at hand and remain motivated by working together. Approaching people when carrying out primary research is also easier with the support of others, especially if you lack confidence, and you will certainly find it easier to ensure no stone goes unturned and questions that need to be answered are not forgotten.

Write up your findings in Word and email the document to your other team members so everyone sees all the results.

LINKS

Here are some examples for publicity approaches used by professional companies. Think about whether any are suitable for you to use. Consider things such as cost, feasibility and availability.

» Word of mouth.

» Advertising – press/TV/radio/posters/leaflets/flyers.

» Sales promotion – e.g. McDonald's Happy Meals.

» Direct marketing – letters to people's houses.

» e-commerce – emailing, websites.

» Internal communications – using the intranet and email network of your centre.

» Exhibitions/displays.

» tele-business – ringing people up.

Some of these techniques are more controversial than others. For example, many people have very strong objections to receiving phonecalls, letters and emails from companies advertising products, and this can often damage your reputation. So be careful how you publicise your product so you don't alienate the audience you are working so hard to encourage to come and see you product.

Some forms of advertising are simply unrealistic for you as they are too expensive. However, a combination of putting up posters and giving out leaflets can be quite cheap and possible to do with the equipment you have at your centre. Placing an advert in the local press might be completely out of the question, but most local newspapers will have a 'What's On' section that is free and you might even be able to encourage the editor to do a news article on your show or exhibition – which is also completely free.

Whatever you plan to do, ensure that the different approaches cover different people and consider what USP you are promoting to the audience you are targeting. A letter or leaflet to parents and teachers telling them about the presentation will be very different from a leaflet advertising the presentation to the general public who won't know you.

Producing and distributing publicity materials

Publicity needs to satisfy the customer. This may seem a weird word to use – satisfy. But you will find that the publicity for a product can sometimes be about something other than what the product actually is. This is done to try to make the product more attractive to an audience.

For example, a car is a collection of metal and plastic that gets you from A to B, but advertising has always made the car out to be so much more: a relationship, a romance, a lifestyle, a fashion statement.

The advertising industry talks about AIDA – **A**ttract, gain **I**nterest, create **D**esire and finally obtain **A**ction. So it's a good idea to bear these aims in mind when designing your own publicity. It needs to instantly connect with your audience, not put them off. You have to catch their eye so they will give your leaflet, poster or even a banner on a website a second look and want to find out more. So your publicity needs to be attractive, appealing and relevant.

FIGURE 5.5 **Clever advertising makes out the product to be so much more than the sum of its parts**

ALL NEW FREELANDER 2
READY WHEN YOU ARE

It's really important that your publicity also includes the correct information needed for someone to fully understand when, where and how to come and see your presentation. A fantastic free article in your local newspaper about your show is useless unless it clearly states the dates and times of the show, where it is being performed and how you can get tickets.

A very common mistake is to have discrepancies between different publicity materials regarding the information about the presentation. So make sure the whole team are clear on:

» what the presentation is

» who is involved

» when the presentation it taking place

» where it is taking place

» how and where to get tickets

» how much tickets cost, including any variation for children, students, senior citizens and so forth

» where people can get further information, such as a website, email address or telephone number.

Consider using these promotional materials or activities.

» Press release or feature in a local newspaper.

» Leaflets/flyers.

» Posters.

» Advertisements e.g. on your centre's intranet, local paper or radio.

» Display e.g. in the reception of your centre or local library.

Presenting your creative and media work

In completing this unit and finally presenting your product to your audience, it is really important that you continue to be focused on what the audience will be expecting and the experience they will receive when they attend your presentation. What final touches and detail can you make to ensure they have the best, most professional experience?

Completing your tasks

Although this is a group effort it is crucial that you complete your individual tasks to the best of your ability and on time. Try to keep on top of what has been decided in meetings and the impact this might have on you and what you are trying to do. Make sure your voice is heard if someone else's actions or lack of action affect your ability to complete your tasks.

Be realistic. It's better to be honest and warn the group if you are not going to hit a deadline than to stay quiet and hope they won't notice. Hopefully there will be a real team spirit and you will all be supportive of one another if problems arise.

JOURNAL TIPS

Don't forget to record in your Journal what you have completed, when you completed it and reflect on how well you have done.

Final preparations

Installing work can take hours, days or even weeks, depending on what you are doing. Never underestimate how long it takes to hang pictures, put up sets and prepare for any type of presentation – you will find you never have enough time!

It is really important that you are systematic about how you install your presentation in a room, theatre or gallery. Don't all pile in with your work and start installing individually. Think through the process of what needs to be achieved first. You may find that you want your product nowhere near the room until you have properly set up everything else. If you are trying to recreate a gallery space you might need an emptied room and panels for hanging the pictures on. The room might need clearing, cleaning, hoovering and even painting. The panels may have to be constructed and painted actually in the room. You don't want to be doing this while all your finished work lies around at risk of getting damaged.

MANAGE

When managing projects you need to demonstrate that you can organise your time effectively, ensuring that resources are suitable and available when you require them, and that you can prioritise your tasks.

Try writing each task and action that needs to take place on an individual piece of paper. Lay the pieces of paper out on a table, and start to organise them in the order of completion. What needs to be done first? What next? What last?

Having the tasks on pieces of paper means you can keep moving things about until you find the best order. You can also add more actions or tasks as you think of them. Write down tasks that others are doing that directly affect you on different coloured paper and fit them into the scheme. You will be able to see instantly how these affect your tasks.

Once you are happy with it, write it down or take a photo of it. Record in your Journal whether or not you kept to your order and if this exercise helped you manage your tasks.

Upload your photo onto a computer and print it out as large as you can. You can then pin it up somewhere for easy reference.

LINKS

If you are carrying out a **get-in** for a theatre show then there would be a very clear order of things that need to be done:

1. Rig lighting.
2. Rig sound.
3. Rig set and curtains.
4. Focus lighting.
5. Touch up painting.
6. Sort props and furniture.
7. Rig special effects.
8. Technical rehearsal.
9. Dress rehearsal.
10. Performance.

Think how you could learn from this process to successfully rig your presentation, whatever shape or form it may take.

SAFETY TIP

You also need to build safety checks into this schedule. Look back at Units 3 and 4 for more about health and safety issues.

Problem solving

It's important to realise that however much you might prepare and believe you have thought of everything, unexpected problems can still arise and you will have to deal with them effectively.

If the problems arise when your audience is around you need to act swiftly and quietly – there is nothing worse than seeing someone running around in a panic. Stay calm, get help and delegate.

If problems ever involve health and safety issues then you must always ensure that you talk to a member of staff straight away. Never take risks, it is better to be safe than sorry, so if the start of the show needs to be delayed or your exhibition needs to be closed while you sort out the problem – then do it.

Finally

It's always good to have a dress rehearsal, or a dry run, even for an exhibition or an online event. Get people you know, maybe other students, to try out the presentation and feed back comments to you. You may still have time to change things if something isn't working. There is nothing worse than a website that doesn't work on other computers, so test it before the presentation, or get someone else to.

Most importantly ensure that the venue is safe for your audience. Your teacher will be able to help with this, but do carry out risk assessments. Here are some potential problems to think about. You must make sure that:

» there are no trip hazards or things sticking out that might catch on audience's clothes

» there is enough light for the audience to walk around the presentation safely

» noise levels are not too loud so as to damage hearing

» the content of the presentation is suitable for the audience. If there is anything unsuitable for younger audiences you must make this clear beforehand.

At your work experience placement try to find out:

» How the company present its products/services?

» Which staff members organise presentations?

» What skills they need?

I want to be...

...an account manager

» How did you get your job of account manager with advertising agency Team Saatchi?

I was offered a job with the company while I was with them on work experience during the summer before I had even finished my degree course. I had no formal training for the job apart from a Marketing Management module as part of my course. I was judged on my commitment and skills demonstrated through my work experience placement.

» What is an account manager?

Team Saatchi creates advertising across all media platforms from digital to TV and press. As an account manager I am responsible for managing the creative process from briefing to delivery. I provide the first point of contact for clients throughout this process.

» Do you work in a team?

Each account has a team of people assigned to it. In my role I liaise with the creative teams, strategic planners, creative services managers, producers and other account handlers at various levels of the company.

» At what stage in the creative process do you get involved?

I see through the development of a campaign from start to finish, ensuring the efficient delivery of high-quality work within budget and on time.

» What's the hardest thing about your job?

Keeping an overview of the status of the creative process on each account and maintaining a thorough knowledge of my clients' businesses. Being able to switch my attention quickly between different tasks.

» What creative/technical skills do you need to be a good account manager?

Basic word-processing, spreadsheet and PowerPoint skills. Good time-management, presentation skills and the ability to communicate clearly and concisely with people in different roles and at different levels within and outside the business.

» What is the biggest influence on your creative and development decisions?

Aligning creative development with the brand of the company, while balancing financial and planning elements of the brief.

www.teamsaatchi.co.uk

✳ Henry Gray

153

Case Study

Guildford House Gallery →

Guildford House is a 17th-century town house that was turned into an art gallery in 1959.

From April 2005 to March 2006 a record 122,622 visitors came through the doors of Guildford House. These visitors were a combination of local schoolchildren, residents and tourists. So the gallery needs to take into account a wide variety of tastes and interests. As for all local galleries the involvement of the community is vital, so the gallery exhibits local artists as well as hosting touring exhibitions.

Facilities

Exhibition space is provided in the rooms of the main house and also in The Brew House situated in the courtyard at the back.

Personnel

The gallery is run by a Gallery Manager, an Audience Development Officer and a Marketing Administration Officer who are responsible for different aspects of mounting and co-ordinating gallery events and exhibitions.

Types of exhibitions mounted

» Guildford Arts Society – local artists

» Surrey Photographic Association

» Borough Collection – work that has been collected over many years within the Borough of Guildford

» Peter Blake – touring exhibition of the pop artist's work.

Mounting an exhibition or event

Gallery staff have to pull in and co-ordinate all the relevant people involved in putting on an exhibition or event. These are some of the aspects they have to consider:

» theme, timescale and budget

» contacting/commissioning artists to obtain the work

» staging/exhibition layout

» audience interpretation – such as talks from artists, gallery lectures, teachers' packs, guided tours

» marketing, press releases and design of publicity, such as posters/postcards/brochures

» risk assessments for health and safety requirements.

For more information: http://www.guildford.gov.uk/ and follow the links to Guildford House.

Questions

» Find out about your local gallery, what are the roles of the staff in the gallery?

» What does the role of curator involve?

» Describe one of the exhibitions that has recently been put on; who was its target audience?

» How far in advance does the gallery plan its programme?

» What is MLA accreditation?

» What arts and crafts organisations in your area are exhibited in your local gallery, and how are these advertised?

» What role would a graphic designer have in mounting an exhibition?

Assessment Tips

Although this unit will be assessed by your teacher, it is important to remember that it is linked to the Unit 6 Skills Report, which is externally assessed and requires your work within this unit to feed your responses. It is therefore essential to keep careful notes of any ideas, plans and decisions and records of all meetings you have attended, including any site visits to industry venues.

Your Journal should document your ideas and reflections, including reasons for making decisions during the unit. Although you are likely to have worked within a team for this unit, and therefore been assigned a role, or roles, to carry out, you must ensure that you have, and can demonstrate, an understanding of the overall plan and strategy for the presentation. All group work must be written up individually and you must make sure your contribution during the process is clear so it can be assessed.

All your work must be presented in a Process Portfolio and should include the following.

» Notes – research, planning and preparation.

» Your own minutes for all meetings (although this could be included in your Journal). If you used separate sheets make sure that they are in date order.

» Notes on ideas for publicity materials.

» Sketches, drafts and finished examples of publicity materials.

» Notes on setting up for the presentation. This could include plans of the venue showing where everything was set up – the more detailed the better – including revisions and the actual set up used.

» Health and safety issues and how they were dealt with. This could include a risk assessment of the final venue.

Your teacher's notes and records that contribute to assessment will also be given to you to include in the Process Portfolio. These include information on your attendance and punctuality.

SUMMARY / SKILLS CHECK

» Planning your presentation

You should know:

- ✔ what a presentation is and the possibilities available to present your product in an appropriate way
- ✔ how to plan your presentation and run meetings that are productive
- ✔ how to keep proper records of meetings
- ✔ how to work successfully in a team by listening and giving and receiving criticism effectively
- ✔ how to research the venue or location for your presentation
- ✔ how to negotiate the venue to ensure you have the correct facilities and equipment
- ✔ how to prepare for the day
- ✔ how to ensure that your finished product is ready to be presented.

» Publicising your presentation

You should know:

- ✔ what publicity is and understand the USP for your product
- ✔ how to explore the ways in which media events are publicised
- ✔ how to find suitable ways to publicise your presentation and plan your promotional activities
- ✔ how to produce and distribute publicity materials.

» Presenting your creative and media product

You should be able to:

- ✔ perform or complete relevant tasks to the best of your ability
- ✔ prepare the facilities and install the work effectively
- ✔ problem-solve
- ✔ ensure that your presentation is ready for an audience, including whether it is safe.

OVERVIEW

This unit is very different from all the others for two main reasons. Firstly, it is purely about you reflecting on what you have already done in previous units and does not expect you to produce any further creative and media work. Secondly, it is externally assessed, which means that nothing you do for this unit will be assessed or graded by your teachers, it will all be sent off to Edexcel for grading, a bit like a traditional written exam. However, don't panic, as you'll see it is very different from written exams you may have done before, and we will explain how to respond to the questions.

This unit expects you to think about and describe the skills, techniques, materials and production processes involved in the creation of the piece of work from Unit 2, Unit 3 or Unit 4. However, it has to be the *same* work you presented in Unit 5. You will then need to describe how you presented it and finally consider the skills you have developed and what job roles within the real world those skills might be needed for.

Throughout this book you have been told to keep careful records in your Process Portfolio of your creative ideas, how your work has developed and evaluations of finished work. These records will be vital for you to achieve good grades within all the units that make up your course. If you have been careful to keep a detailed Process Portfolio, this will help you prepare for the written paper that is set for Unit 6.

It is important to stress that although this unit is about reflecting on work you have already done, it does not mean that it is only for exam purposes. Time to reflect on products and presentations is crucial for any professional to help them progress within the creative and media industry. The skills that you will be asked to demonstrate in this unit are therefore very important to your future at higher education levels and in the industry. The ability to analyse and learn from successes and failures makes a huge difference to someone's employability and ultimately the salary they can command, so take this unit seriously!

06

Skills Report

Skills list

At the end of this unit you should:

» be able to reflect on how techniques, skills and materials have been used

» be able to reflect on presentation techniques and skills

» know the specific skills required for specific job roles.

Job watch

This unit is relevant to creative and media job roles across the board, including:

» producer
» designer
» writer
» director
» artist/illustrator
» performer
» technician
» administrator.

Introduction

The Skills Report you are being asked to complete has three sections and a total of seven questions. It asks you to reflect on what has already happened – thinking deeply and carefully about it – and then describe the process.

If you don't enjoy exams don't panic! For the Level 1 Creative and Media Diploma the Skills Report is not like a normal exam paper. It contains seven straightforward questions that are given to you in advance. In fact the questions you will have to answer are even in this book, and we will look at them one by one to help you understand how to prepare.

You are also given a generous two hours to complete the Skills Report and, although you have to complete it under exam conditions, you are allowed to take your notes, Process Portfolio and other relevant work into the room. The two hours can also be split into shorter sessions depending on your centre.

The Skills Report is divided into three sections:

» Section A – Reflect on work you have produced that has then been presented.

» Section B – Reflect on your presentation skills and techniques.

» Section C – Know the skills required for specific job roles.

We will now look at each section and give you some helpful hints on how to prepare for completing your Skills Report.

FIGURE 6.1 **Reflecting on your work is all part of the job for a creative and media professional**

How you created the work (Section A)

Before you start preparing for this part of the Skills Report, make sure you fully understand which work you will be talking about. You will have completed two units out of: Unit 2: Visual Arts, Unit 3: Performance Arts and Unit 4: Media Production, and presented the work of one of these units for Unit 5: Presentation. It is *this* work that you must now consider in more detail. For Section A of the Skills Report you are concerned about how the work was *created*, not how it was *presented* – that's for Section B.

There are two questions in Section A.

TRY THIS

If you are still unsure, ask your teacher. Have your Process Portfolio handy to help you prepare for answering the Skills Report questions.

How was the work created?

Whether you created the work individually or within a group, first of all you need to consider the processes that led up to the creation of the finished product. Here is the actual question 1 you will be answering.

FIGURE 6.2 **Section A Question 1**

1 Describe as clearly as you can how you created the work which you presented for Unit 5.

You should describe what you did, the materials or technology you used, and the techniques and skills you used.

You should describe what you did in the order in which you did things.

If you worked in a group you should describe first what the group as a whole did, and then what you yourself did.

[You should aim to write around 200 words for this section]

Response

You will notice from the way the Skills Report is written that each question is followed by more detail about what you need to write about, an idea of how many words you should write to satisfy the assessment, and a box for you to type your response into.

It can be a good idea to break down the larger question into several smaller questions. You might find it useful to write your answers under these as sub-headings, which you can either leave in or take out before you submit you finished response.

For this particular question you have to make sure you write down what happened in the order it happened. Include information about the techniques and skills you learnt and the materials and technology you used. However carefully you may have organised your Process Portfolio and Journal you may find you need to spend some time making sure you have got everything in the correct order and haven't left anything out.

Why not draw up a table like the one below to help you order your thoughts? This is an extract from a table by a student who was completing the Advertising and Graphic Design disciplines. Even if you have only skeleton information in the table you will find it really useful to make sure you don't forget anything and ensure that your finished response is not cluttered and is written in a logical order.

TRY THIS

Look through your Process Portfolio and Journal for ideas on what to write about.

TABLE 6.1 Student summary table

	Description	Group or Individual	Materials and/or Technology	What have you learnt?
1.	Brain-storm ideas – Advertising opportunities	Group		Discussion/blue sky thinking
2.	Research leaflets and graphic design software	Individual	Internet, Photoshop InDesign	Research techniques, graphics manipulation, basic page layout
3.	Group meeting – Group agreed to create a leaflet after listening to my presentation	Group, Individual	PowerPoint	Presentation skills to present research on creating leaflets
4.	Research suitable photographs and images for the leaflet	Individual	Internet, books, professional leaflets	Research techniques. Through looking at professional leaflets for similar products I learnt what style my leaflet should have, the kind of images that were suitable and what font I wanted to use

If you are using software on a computer to create your table then it's really simple to add or insert a line if you realise you have forgotten something.

Research

The second question for Section A asks you to reflect on the background research you carried out.

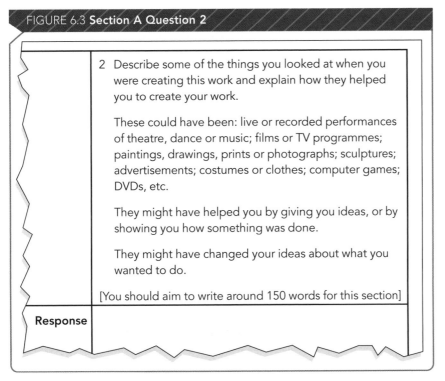

FIGURE 6.3 **Section A Question 2**

2 Describe some of the things you looked at when you were creating this work and explain how they helped you to create your work.

These could have been: live or recorded performances of theatre, dance or music; films or TV programmes; paintings, drawings, prints or photographs; sculptures; advertisements; costumes or clothes; computer games; DVDs, etc.

They might have helped you by giving you ideas, or by showing you how something was done.

They might have changed your ideas about what you wanted to do.

[You should aim to write around 150 words for this section]

Response

To be successful in responding to this question you must make sure you don't simply write about the things you looked at. Writing 150 words on the TV programmes you watched doesn't tell an examiner how they helped you develop your ideas.

Make sure you answer the question – what have you *learnt* from your knowledge of other people's work and your wider understanding of the type of products you were creating? You need to state how things you have seen influenced you, gave you ideas or demonstrated professional practice.

REFLECT

Consider the items you used in your research (for instance TV programmes, live performances or magazine articles) one at a time and write brief notes about what you learnt from each one and how it affected your finished product. Did it confirm or help you develop your ideas or did it change your mind about something completely?

How you presented the work (Section B)

You are now asked to reflect on the *presentation* of the work, and *not* the work itself. You may find, however, that some research done during the making of the product might come in handy for answering some of the following questions about your presentation, especially questions concerning your audience.

There are four questions in Section B.

Reflect on planning your presentation

The first question asks you to describe and reflect on how you planned your presentation. It is likely that you planned the presentation within a group and you will need to make this clear and describe what the group did, but you must also ensure that it is clear what you did *individually* and what particular roles you carried out.

FIGURE 6.4 **Section B Question 1**

1 Describe your preparations for the presentation of your work.

You should set out your planning process, and show how closely you followed those plans.

Your response could include flowcharts and diagrams.

If you worked in a group you must describe what the group did and your own contribution to the process.

[You should aim to write around 150 words for this section]

Response

Examples of planning decisions that you will have made are:

» Venue – size, location, cost.

» Resources – staging, chairs, screens.

» Equipment – projectors, computers, lighting, sound.

» Tickets – price.

» Publicity materials – what promotions did you carry out and when?

Make sure you outline the kinds of meetings that took place and the decisions that were made. You don't have many words here to describe a lot of detail, so remember that a picture or diagram can say a lot. Consider using diagrams or flow charts to help you describe the processes, this will make it a lot clearer for the examiner.

Remember, you can include other documents with your Skills Report, so make sure you have things such as pictures of the presentation or ground plans with you when you are writing the Skills Report to ensure you explain and refer to the extra files correctly.

This example of a flowchart is an extract from a student who was organising a presentation of a short film:

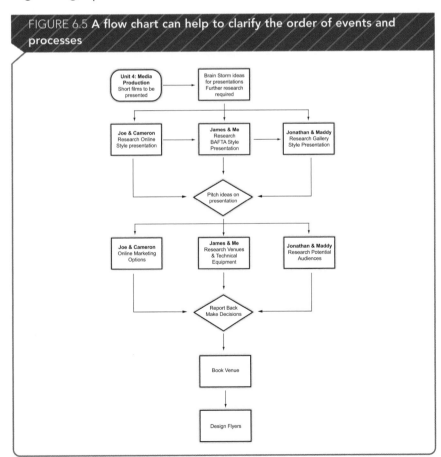

FIGURE 6.5 **A flow chart can help to clarify the order of events and processes**

FIGURE 6.6 **Careful preparations and attention to detail help ensure the success of a media product**

Target audience

FIGURE 6.7 **Section B Question 2**

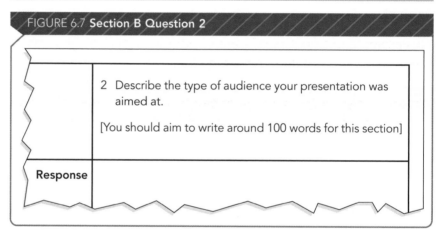

2 Describe the type of audience your presentation was aimed at.

[You should aim to write around 100 words for this section]

Response

During the making of the product you will have considered your target audience. This research and information should be included when completing your response. However, who you finally publicised your event to might be different so do make sure you consider the bigger picture.

For example, you might have devised a short musical play for primary-school children and researched this particular age group in detail to ensure that the final product was appropriate. However, it won't be the children themselves buying the tickets and taking themselves off to the show, so you need to publicise the event to parents and carers. Therefore the way you plan and deliver your presentation should reflect this. If so, then don't forget to talk about it! Remember you can have several USPs for a single product when you are targeting different parts of your audience.

You must ensure that you are clear about how you considered your audience when planning your presentation, and how this affected your planning and what you eventually delivered.

What did your audience think?

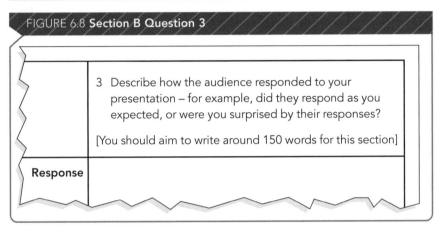

FIGURE 6.8 **Section B Question 3**

> 3 Describe how the audience responded to your presentation – for example, did they respond as you expected, or were you surprised by their responses?
>
> [You should aim to write around 150 words for this section]

Response

To answer Question 3, some kind of research gathering is crucial to help you write something meaningful. Throughout this book, it has been suggested that you always gather feedback in lots of different ways and from different people (360-degree feedback for example), and of course audience feedback is essential to help you understand how you did.

Analysing how your audience responded to your presentation doesn't have to be from them answering a formal questionnaire or being interviewed. If you performed in front of your audience then you will have a very clear idea of how they responded to your work. Did they laugh in the right places? Were they quiet during the important emotional parts? If you were running a gallery you may have found that your audience commented to you as they left or you may have gone over and spoken to them as they walked around. However, try to make sure that when you gather this feedback that you don't ruin their experience of your presentation. No one likes a pushy salesperson who continually comes up and asks whether you need help when you just want to enjoy looking!

If you have little feedback when you come to prepare for this question then why not think about contacting students and staff that did come to see your presentation and get some feedback by asking them to complete a questionnaire or join a break-time discussion which you can video. And don't forget to ask the others in your team.

Reflect on working safely

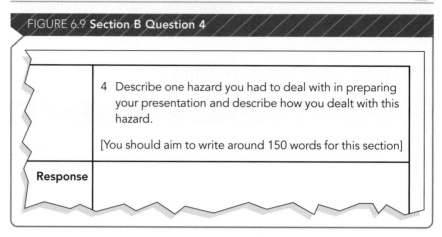

FIGURE 6.9 **Section B Question 4**

> 4 Describe one hazard you had to deal with in preparing your presentation and describe how you dealt with this hazard.
>
> [You should aim to write around 150 words for this section]
>
> **Response**

You are only asked to comment on *one* hazard; however you should aim to write 150 words, therefore it is important that you go into enough detail to satisfy the assessment. For example, if you are writing about manual-handling hazards (lifting heavy equipment) you need to go into a little more detail than simply stating that you all were careful not to lift anything heavy! What is regarded as being too heavy? What can be lifted by one person and what needs two? Does the shape of what is being lifted change the decision? How much of a problem was lifting heavy items during the planning and running of your presentation? Once you knew it might be a problem what steps did you take to ensure that no one did get hurt, for example did you:

» decide on what couldn't be lifted alone

» have someone take responsibility for monitoring what people carried

» ensure that everyone understood the restrictions for healthy working?

Working at heights is also a very good subject to talk about, as is electrical safety. You should have checked out some of the government websites for more information on health and safety issues as part of Unit 5. Use this work, or revisit the websites, to help you talk more knowledgeably and constructively about health and safety issues.

Know the skills for specific job roles (Section C)

As you created your media product you will have used techniques and skills that professionally trained people from the industry get paid to have and apply. These people have specific job roles and titles, and this is what you will need to research and know about to successfully answer the final questions in the Skills Report.

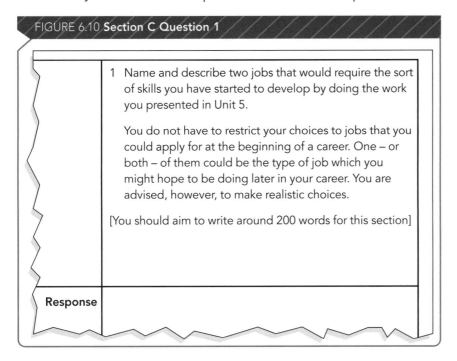

FIGURE 6.10 **Section C Question 1**

1 Name and describe two jobs that would require the sort of skills you have started to develop by doing the work you presented in Unit 5.

You do not have to restrict your choices to jobs that you could apply for at the beginning of a career. One – or both – of them could be the type of job which you might hope to be doing later in your career. You are advised, however, to make realistic choices.

[You should aim to write around 200 words for this section]

Response

You need to talk about two job roles that require the kinds of skills you will have started to use and develop in the making of your creative and media product.

You might have produced a short film as part of a team, with your specific duties being operating the camera. Therefore you might choose to discuss the job roles of camera operator and film director. Although the film director doesn't necessarily do any filming, they do need to understand the skills and techniques of the cameras so they can communicate with the film crew to get the shots that they want.

You may have carried out several roles during the creation of your product and decide to look at two of these roles. For example, if you have taken part in a performance as a dancer you may also have had to work out the dance moves yourself, in the real world this would have been done by two different people, the first to work out the dance routine – the choreographer – and the second to learn and perform it – the dancer. Both require similar fundamental skills and techniques in terms of understanding the dance discipline they are working within, but they also involve different skills: one to create the dance, the other to interpret it.

You need to research what all these skills are. Look back at what you did in Unit 1 about job roles and writing a skills audit for each of the roles. Many of the job roles you will be researching are advertised every day in local and national papers and on websites. Ideally it would be great to get hold of an actual job description for a specific role that is being advertised in the industry. This is not as hard as you might think. Many creative and media roles are advertised, for example through the *Guardian* newspaper or online. Why not check out http://jobs.guardian.co.uk/? If you look at these job descriptions you will see clear lists of essential and desirable skills.

Some job roles are not advertised as they are usually given to people on recommendation or after seeing their work. For example, the role of director (either theatre or film) would not usually be advertised in a newspaper. However, you will find grants and awards for new and up-and-coming directors that will give you a clear idea about what people are looking for and the skills that are important. Don't forget – 'life' skills are also important for some job roles.

What's a realistic choice of job role to consider?
It's probably realistic to talk about the general skills needed to direct a film, but not the specific skills to direct a Hollywood blockbuster. Think job roles rather than specific people. For example, although you might want to have a career similar to Steven Spielberg or Andrew Lloyd Webber, citing their individual skills lists would be unsuitable as they are so individual; not many film directors or composers of musicals have successful careers as producers at the same time and, in the case of Spielberg, run a successful animation and special effects company too. However, to look at the skills needed to be a successful film director or producer, or a composer or producer of musicals would be sensible. This would also mean that you have indirectly looked at two specific job roles, which meets the assessment needs of the question.

FIGURE 6.11 **Steven Spielberg's career spans writing, directing, producing and running a company**

Electronic Skills Report and attaching files

As previously mentioned, if you are not careful you might easily run out of space to respond to the questions. If you feel you need to write more than is recommended you may do so, as you will not be penalised in this assessment for going over the recommended number of words. However, make sure that everything you write is absolutely relevant, that you are not using words wastefully and that you are not just repeating yourself.

Sometimes things can be quite complicated to explain in words and it helps both you and the examiner if you can show examples instead. You are therefore allowed to attach electronic files to be read alongside your Skills Report. Typically these will be pictures, graphs and/or plans to help explain things in fewer words. But remember, these files should not simply be another 200-word report continuing on from where you finished on the exam paper!

Any files you wish to include with your Skills Report need to be prepared in advance of the exam. Many of these files will take some time to sort out and you need to make sure they work on all computers. It's very important, therefore, that you give yourself enough time to ensure they are properly formatted. Your teacher will help you with the formats and sizes of these files.

All your files (including your Skills Report) will be collected together in one folder that will be sent to Edexcel. Make sure your file names for your extra work are sensible and correctly named within your Skills Report. For example, it is an excellent idea to use your candidate number as part of the file name.

File formats

A number of file formats are acceptable as attachments in you Skills Report. But please note that Word documents are *not* acceptable. However, with most software you can create a PDF version by selecting 'Print' and, instead of sending the document to the printer select 'Save as PDF'. If your computer or software doesn't have this function then you can send your text document as an RTF or EPS file, which ensures that the file can be read by any computer.

Acceptable file formats are:

» RTF for text files

» EPS for text files with images, but only if there is no other option

» PDF for text files that can include photos and scans

» JPEG for image files – photos/drawings/scanned artwork, etc.

» MP3 for sound files – music/songs/sound effects, etc.

   – AIFF file format is also acceptable as this is industry-standard quality. However you can only use audio clips up to two-minutes long

» FLV (preferred) or MPEG for video files – video, multimedia, animation, etc.

» HTML for web pages

   – However, to ensure that the HTML page is complete with graphics, logos and animations, etc. you will need to ensure that all these files are also included within the folder

   – If you just want the examiner to see the web pages, but they don't have to work, then it is a good idea to produce a PDF version or screen shot of the web page than to try and put the entire working website with your Skills Report.

I want to be...

... creative

» How would you describe your current employment in the creative and media industry?

Together with my husband David, I sing, coach, present, write and mentor.

» What work have you recently been involved in?

We created and performed in the new CBeebies series *Carrie & David's Popshop*, making music for the under-fives. We are involved with the government's plans for developing singing in schools and we use singing to teach high-profile business leaders about strategy and change for their companies. We were also coaches for *Pop Idol*, *Fame Academy* and *The One and Only*.

» What training did you have before working in the industry?

Trained and took examinations for ballet, tap and jazz. Trained with leading vocal coaches to develop and learn about the voice. There is no greater training than work itself.

» What's the hardest thing about your job?

The zillion little bits of administration that go into achieving one creative project. It's not enough to just be creative in this industry. You have to be able to create a structure whereby your creative gifts can flourish.

» What creative, technical or personal skills do you most value?

People skills. Without these all the rest means nothing. You have to have a level of creative skills but in our industry what you're like to work with will have the biggest impact on whether you get re-booked.

» What qualities do you look for in the people you work with?

Loyalty and a desire to learn.

» What is the biggest influence on your creative decisions?

I divide our creative activity into commercial creativity and spontaneous creativity. Commercial creativity is influenced by the question – who is this for? Once we know our audience we then tailor the product to this. Our spontaneous creativity is influenced only by whatever is going on in our internal world and a desire to express that.

» What one piece of advice would you give someone thinking of a creative and media career?

Who are you? Once you know, express the answer to this question fearlessly. If you are honest others will relate to you. People respond to truth.

✳ Carrie Grant

Assessment Tips

This is a written exam with time restraints; however don't panic, as the time given for you to complete the Skills Report is quite generous. You are unlikely to feel the pressures of a traditional exam, especially as the completion of the Skills Report will take place in a computer suite where you type your answers into the question paper rather than writing by hand. However, it is required that you:

» write your responses directly into the electronic paper entirely on your own

» are supervised and will work under exam conditions in which you are not able to talk to anyone else except the invigilator

» will not have access to the Internet during the exam.

Although you have to type straight into the electronic paper, you are able to edit as you go and can therefore correct mistakes before submitting your final responses. Spell checkers are a way of life and used throughout the industry, however use them with caution. Often people will simply choose the wrong word from the list when correcting. Make sure you know how to spell technical terms and names as no spell checker will recognise these. Also remember that spell checkers will not pick up words that are correctly spelled but are still mistakes – for instance if you mistyped 'form' instead of 'from' – so try to leave enough time to proofread your work at the end of the exam.

Good punctuation, spelling and a clear professional writing style are crucial so that the examiner can clearly recognise your understanding and doesn't have to wade through unclear or badly written English. Don't use text abbreviations or write as if you are chatting to your mates on MSN; this is a Skills Report, a professional document just like any other professional report you would come across in the industry. Treat it with respect and take care with its appearance and clarity.

As it's a report, you can use bullet points and sub-headings for longer questions. This actually makes it easier for the examiner to navigate through your answer and check you have covered all the necessary points.

Most questions suggest that you write between 100 and 200 words. This is not a lot and you will find that you can write a lot more than this very quickly if you are well prepared. It's a really good idea to try answering the questions on your own before the exam, so you can get used to writing within the constraints of the word count. However, remember you are only allowed to take into the exam room your notes, Process Portfolio and Journal – not pre-prepared answers.

As the seven questions are published within the qualification specification, you will have plenty of time to discuss them with your teacher prior to the exam to ensure that you fully understand them and what is being asked for. However, your teachers are not allowed to help you structure your answers or give you specific advice on your responses either before you go into the exam or during it.

If you are properly prepared, follow the guidance in this book, and walk into the exam room with a detailed Process Portfolio and Journal then you should have no problem in responding to the questions. In fact, your main problem will probably be ensuring that you don't write too much!

FIGURE 6.12 **Remember you can take in your Journal to help you with your Skills Report**

To achieve the higher grades

To achieve the higher grades you should:

» give detailed and clear responses

» make clear what you did as an individual

» put everything in the correct order

» give examples of the work of two or more professionals and show how it influenced your work.

SUMMARY / SKILLS CHECK

» Reflect on how you created previous work (Skills Report – Section A)

You should know how to describe:

- ✓ how your work was created, whether individually or as a group
- ✓ what you learnt as a result of completing the work – including technical skills, performance skills and knowledge about similar work done by other professional creative and media people
- ✓ what you learnt from looking at similar work done by other industry figures, both past and present.

» Reflect on how you presented the work (Skills Report – Section B)

You should be able to describe how:

- ✓ you planned your presentation – including researching the venue/location, holding meetings and making decisions
- ✓ you considered your audience when planning your presentation
- ✓ your audience responded to your presentation
- ✓ you ensured you were working safely at all times by stating one hazard and describing how you dealt with it.

» Know the skills for specific job roles (Skills Report – Section C)

You should know how:

- ✓ to name and describe two job roles that would have required the same sort of skills to complete the work in the professional world.

Glossary

360-degree feedback   feedback on your work from all sides, e.g. clients, colleagues, bosses, audience

acoustics   the sound qualities of a room or space. The acoustics of a room, concert hall or theatre can affect the original sound, for instance by adding reverberation (echo – like in a church)

advance   an amount of money given to someone contracted to create a product, such as an album or book, to help them get started. This money is then taken off the money earned by the product in **royalties**

agenda   a list of items to be discussed or decisions to be made at a meeting. The agenda is usually distributed to the people attending several days before the meeting

aims   long-term goals. Often used with **objectives**, short-term goals

amateur   someone who creates a media product but is not paid to do it

analyse   to examine something in depth or detail

angel   an investor in West End shows who provides enough funding to create and present a play or musical. They are known as angels because the investment can be extremely high-risk

applied learning   learning that applies theory to practice, putting knowledge to hands-on use

aural   to do with listening. An aural learner, for instance, takes in information best from things they hear

blog   an online journal

centre   a generic term used by Edexcel for the place where you are being taught your Creative and Media Diploma. It could be a school, college or place of work

commission   a request from a client to do a specific job to the client's requirements, usually for an agreed fee

competencies   things that you do well and efficiently

concept map   visual representation of your ideas that you have drawn. Also known as pattern notes or a mind map

context   the background to an event, statement or idea, that helps it to be fully understood

contingency   an amount of money that is added to a production's budget in case of emergencies – e.g. if something ended up costing more than had been budgeted for, filming having been postponed due to bad weather so cameras had to be hired for an extra day, etc. Can also refer to additional time built into a schedule in case problems arise

cue sheet   a list of signals (cues) for something to happen in performance art. These can be visual or part of a script indicating when a particular action must happen

CV   short for Curriculum Vitae, which is a description of a person's background to send to companies when applying for work. Typically it includes personal details, such as address, and date of birth, as well as education details, qualifications and previous jobs and experience

evaluation   assessing what was achieved, what was good and what was not, and how things could be improved

experiential learning   learning by doing and experiencing oneself rather than theoretically from books or the experiences of others

feasible   how possible something will be to produce and market in terms of cost, resources, likely sales, etc.

franchise   a company or individual licensed to sell goods or services for another individual or company

freelance   a person who sells their expertise or services to different companies at different times, rather than being employed permanently with one company

get-in   the process of moving the scenery, lighting, sound and other equipment into a venue, such as a concert hall or theatre

idea storm   thinking of all the possible ways to solve a problem or meet a creative brief before making a decision

location recce   a first visit to check if a location is appropriate for filming, recording or performance

maquette   a scale model. Used by sculptors, prop makers, etc. to try out their ideas on a small scale. A good way to avoid costly mistakes by making a smaller version first

milestone   an event or time in your schedule when something has to be completed by or happen. For example, when words have to be learnt by during rehearsals or when filming has to be completed by before editing can start

minutes   notes taken as an accurate record of a meeting specifically detailing decisions and actions agreed. Normally distributed to all attendees after the meeting and approved by them

montage   a technique of producing a new product from existing fragments of pictures, text, sound or film

mood-board   visual representations of a creative concept, used to show how a final product will look

narrative   story or background theme that runs through a media product

objective (1)   a specific outcome you are aiming to achieve

objective (2)   being able to consider ideas and opinions without allowing personal feelings to influence decisions

op art   art that uses optical illusion

plagiarise   to use others' work and pass it off as yours or not acknowledge it

pointillism   a drawing or painting style that builds up the image using dots

pop art   a style of art inspired by commercial and popular culture, for example, television, pop music, advertising, comic books, etc.

product   something that is made for consumption

production process   the method of creating a product

production schedule   the planned timeline for the production process, showing when each step will take place

proposal   brief description of a planned product or project put forward to a client for consideration

rational   being able to think in a reasonable and sensible way – clearly and logically

risk assessment   an official document completed before activities take place to consider whether there are any hazards for the people involved and whether steps can be take to reduce the likelihood or severity of these hazards

royalties   a percentage of the money earned by a product given back to the creator of the product, e.g. the artist/author/musician, etc.

schematic (for website)   a diagram that represents the various pages of a website, showing the links that make the navigation work

shooting script   a comprehensive script, including camera positions and angles, stage directions and lighting directions

skills audit   assessment of the skills you have with a view to identifying gaps in your knowledge

story-board   a sequence of drawings, often with directions and dialogue, used to demonstrate how the film, play or other narrative unfolds

subjective   where someone is influenced more by their own feelings about something than by actual fact

target audience   the audience a particular media product is being made for

transferable skills   generic skills in English, maths, ICT, thinking and learning that are applicable in all walks of life

trapping   when you capture fibres/threads, etc. between fabrics that are transparent or within plastics or any kind of see-through material

treatment   a document developed from a proposal that provides more detail. It might include director's intentions, costs, timescales and staff that may be used in the production

underwrite   where an individual or a company will step in and finance a project or product if it fails to make a profit and loses money

USP   Unique Selling Point of a product that makes it different from similar products

Index